Making Smart Decisions

The Results-Driven Manager Series

The Results-Driven Manager series collects timely articles from *Harvard Management Update*, *Harvard Management Communication Letter*, and the *Balanced Scorecard Report* to help senior to middle managers sharpen their skills, increase their effectiveness, and gain a competitive edge. Presented in a concise, accessible format to save managers valuable time, these books offer authoritative insights and techniques for improving job performance and achieving immediate results.

Other books in the series:

Teams That Click

Presentations That Persuade and Motivate

Face-to-Face Communications for Clarity and Impact

Winning Negotiations That Preserve Relationships

Managing Yourself for the Career You Want

Getting People on Board

Taking Control of Your Time

Dealing with Difficult People

Managing Change to Reduce Resistance

Becoming an Effective Leader

Motivating People for Improved Performance

Hiring Smart for Competitive Advantage

Retaining Your Best People

A Timesaving Guide

THE RESULTS-DRIVEN MANAGER

Making Smart Decisions

• • •

Harvard Business School Press

Boston, Massachusetts

Printed in the United States of America

12 11 10 09 08   6 5 4 3 2

978-1-4221-0182-7 (ISBN 13)

Library of Congress Cataloging-in-Publication Data

The results driven manager : making smart decisions.
     p. cm. – (The results-driven manager series)
   ISBN 1-4221-0182-7
   1. Industrial management–Decision making. I. Title: Making smart decisions. II. Harvard Business School Press. III. Series.
   HD30.23.R477 2006
   658.4'03–dc22

2005030174

Contents

Contents

Applying Potent Decision Tactics

Combating Cognitive Biases

Leveraging Your Intuition

Introduction

• • •

You face one decision after another in your role as a manager. For example, which of those promising job candidates should you hire? How might you solve that nagging problem of order-fulfillment errors? Should you suggest a brand extension to revive a mature product, or take some other, entirely different course of action? When do you call a halt to your research of potential vendors and select a provider from the available candidates?

To make the situation even more interesting, decision making has grown increasingly challenging for managers and executives at all levels in organizations. Today's pace of change and mounting pressure to generate results force managers to select a course of action quickly, before having all the needed information on hand.

At the same time, the dangers of making a poor decision have never been so high. Select the wrong product strategy, and your company's brand weakens while revenues plummet. Pick the wrong hire, and your group's morale and productivity erode. Launch the wrong initiative to turn an inefficient process around, and mistakes and frustration accumulate.

Conversely, when you make smart decisions, you generate enormous value for your company. A brilliantly developed brand strategy nets your organization a greater share of the market. Selecting the right talent for your project team ensures a successful implementation—delivered on time and within budget. A savvy choice of supplier means that your outsourcing strategy produces the promised benefits: lower costs, more streamlined processes, and more time for managers to focus on strategic, not administrative, concerns.

Smart Choices, Big Benefits

The benefits of smart decision making are clear—and can help your firm achieve the innovation, efficiency, and strategic focus it needs to leave competitors scrambling. But to generate these benefits, you need to find ways to work within the constraints that are an unavoidable reality for today's managers. This means taking a strategic approach to your decision making. For example, there are numerous tried-and-true decision processes out there, and you must select the one that best fits your situation. A decision process appropriate and useful for planning a project may backfire if you apply that same process to making a tough ethical call.

Moreover, every decision poses risks: You assemble the right project team, only to see a key member of the team go out on medical leave during a crucial stage in the project. You finally choose a vendor for your outsourcing project, and the company proves unable to deliver the high level of service you expected. You develop a great marketing campaign, and discover that customers have changed their minds about what they want from your company and industry. Strategic decision making must include a clear-eyed assessment of the risks inherent in the various alternatives you're considering—and the development of effective countermeasures tailored to each type of risk.

In addition, you need to know how to process information while making a decision. That includes identifying which data are relevant to your situation, and which can be ignored. Evaluating the relevance of data can help you avoid "information overload." Processing information effectively also means soliciting the right kind of input from the right people—so you generate the most comprehensive range of options and gain a clear picture of the potential risks and rewards of each.

And while you're processing information, you have to watch for and avoid common cognitive biases that can blindside even the most seasoned managers. These

biases are legion—from downplaying the probable negative consequences of a decision and giving the greatest
weight to the first data you gather, to relying too heavily
on past events to make decisions and feeling overconfident of your judgment's infallibility. As much as we'd
like to believe that decision making can be a completely
rational process, it cannot be—thanks to these all-too-
common mental biases.

Communication also plays a role in savvy decision
making. For instance, examining the rationale behind
your proposed choices to others in your company can
help you spot—and correct—errors in your thinking. And
gathering opposing viewpoints can enable you to identify concerns simmering within your decision stakeholders—those who have an interest in the outcome of your
choice or who would be affected in some way by that
outcome. By identifying your stakeholders' concerns,
you can make decisions that take those concerns into
account—as well as begin winning buy-in for your ideas.

To further strengthen your strategic decision making,
you need to leverage your intuition—that mysterious
capability by which you "know something without
knowing *how* you know it." Despite widespread opinions
to the contrary, intuition can play an important role in
smart decision making. But to use your intuition effectively, you must recognize the types of decisions in
which intuition is most appropriate, ensure your intuition's reliability, and augment your "gut sense" with
cold, hard data before making your final choice.

Decision making is bound to grow only more challenging as the pace of change continues to accelerate and as the pressure to make smart business choices mounts ever higher. But by taking a strategic approach to decision making, you can sweeten the odds of making choices that generate value for your company, your career, and your peers and employees.

The articles in this volume describe potent tools and techniques to help you make smart decisions—with special emphasis on how to select and use the right decision-making process, how to apply valuable decision-making tactics, how to combat cognitive biases, and how to leverage your intuition while making decisions. Here's a preview of what you'll find in the volume's four sections.

Using the Right
Decision-Making Process

Decision processes abound—so how do you select the right one? The articles in this section offer ideas for matching a decision process to the various situations you face as a manager—everything from making basic business decisions and managing projects, to making difficult ethical choices and determining who should have the right to make which decisions.

In the first article, "Problem Solving for Decision Makers," business writer Loren Gary describes a six-step process for making basic business decisions: 1) *Define the problem*. Conduct a broad-based analysis of the factors contributing to the problem you're trying to solve. For example, what's causing sales of a successful product to soften? 2) *Identify your criteria*. Define the objectives you need to accomplish in making the decision at hand. Do you want to boost sales? Increase market share? Enhance profitability? 3) *Weigh your criteria*. Which objectives are the most important? Assign them a number indicating their weight. 4) *Generate alternatives*. Brainstorm a broad range of alternative courses of action that could help you to achieve the objectives you've defined. 5) *Rate each alternative on each criterion*. How well does each alternative course of action satisfy each of your key criteria? Assign each alternative a number indicating its effectiveness. 6) *Compute the optimal decision*. For each alternative, multiply the expected effectiveness of the alternative to each criterion by the weight you've assigned each criterion. The highest score is your most rational choice.

In "Putting Real Options to Work to Improve Project Planning," management consultant Fabian D'Souza shifts the focus from basic business decisions to strategies for making smart choices while managing a project. During many project implementations, managers must make important decisions at key project milestones. D'Souza explains how to use "decision trees" to make the wisest choices at those junctures. For example, if your project involves installing a new technology, an early milestone in the planning process brings up the question of whether to develop the technology over time at a lower cost, or to buy it now at a higher cost. Through the decision-tree process, you analyze the possible outcomes of each choice, and assign a percentage indicating the likelihood that each outcome will come to pass. You weigh the probabilities and select your choice based on your business objectives.

In addition to basic business decisions and project management choices, you may also need to make decisions that have sobering ethical implications. For example, should you accept basketball tickets from a vendor? Tell an employee who's asking you for financial advice that he's about to be laid off? Withhold relevant information while providing a reference? In "How to Make Tough Ethical Calls," Emerson College professor Jeffrey Seglin suggests asking yourself six questions to make the best possible ethical decisions: 1) Why is the decision bothering you? 2) Who else matters in this decision? 3) Is the decision your responsibility? 4) What is the ethical concern? 5) What do others think? 6) Are you being true to yourself?

Sometimes a decision centers on determining who will have the right to make certain types of decisions. In "Put the Right Decisions in the Right Hands," business writer Peter Jacobs lays out a process for allocating decision rights: 1) Review how decision authority is currently distributed in your group. Do decision "owners" have sufficient information to make smart decisions? If not, consider reallocating decision rights. 2) Balance centralization and decentralization of decision making. Involve all key stakeholders, but don't bring so many people into the decision process that things grind to a halt. 3) Ensure that everyone understands unequivocally who has the right to make which decisions. 4) Don't immediately blame decision makers if a good decision produces a bad outcome. Redistributing decision authority requires careful thought. Instead of blaming, find out what went wrong—and address the causes during the next decision.

Applying Potent Decision Tactics

The articles in this section focus on specific tactics you can apply to improve the soundness of your decisions. Business writer Lauren Keller Johnson starts things off with "Debriefing Paul Nutt: Increase the Odds of Being Right." According to Nutt, author of *Why Decisions Fail*, a potent strategy to improve decision making is to expand the range of alternatives under consideration for each decision. By enlarging your "pool" of choices, you avoid the common mistake of seizing the first seemingly good idea that comes along. You thus increase the odds of ultimately picking the best possible choice. To encourage the generation of alternatives, create a "safe space" in which you and your stakeholders can brainstorm freely, without judging one another's ideas. Also study past decisions, analyzing what made them succeed or fail.

Ask, "Where did I miss an opportunity to generate additional alternatives? How can I avoid this mistake while making future decisions?"

But expanding your pool of alternatives is only one part of making decisions. You also need to assess the full range of relevant risks while weighing various options. Management consultant Adrian Slywotzky turns to strategies for assessing decision risk in "What Are the Risks You *Should* Be Taking?" According to Slywotzky, too many managers neglect to consider "strategic risk" while making business decisions. Examples of strategic risk include changes in customers' priorities that can make your company's offerings irrelevant, new technologies that might overtake your product, a misdeed that could cause your brand to collapse, and a one-of-a-kind rival that threatens to render your business model obsolete. Slywotzky offers ideas for countering such risks. For example, use your company's assets and customer relationships to develop new lines of business. And leverage proprietary information to distinguish your company from the competition.

Another helpful decision-making tactic is to effectively weigh the information you have at hand while considering various courses of action. Business editor Paul Michelman offers three guidelines in "What Leaders Allow Themselves to Know": 1) Ensure that you gather information from the people best positioned and qualified to have helpful perspectives—even if their views are difficult to hear or conflict with information you've already gathered. 2) Understand the culture, values, and history of your part of the organization—so you can make decisions that people can embrace and support. 3) Clarify what you know and don't know about yourself. Leaders who lack self-knowledge risk misinterpreting and misusing decision-related data available to them.

Business writer Nick Morgan's "Put Your Decision Making to the Test: Communicate" offers additional ideas for improving your decision skills. For example, don't allow others to rush you into a decision. Make the choice when you're ready. If events force a decision on you, try to keep your options open as much and as long as possible. In addition, break big decisions into several little ones. For instance, if you're trying to decide whether to relocate to take a new job, don't commit to one irrevocable path (moving) or another (staying put). Instead, decide to take a week's vacation in the new town, so you can research the business climate and get familiar with the area and its offerings. You'll be taking a smaller, more manageable step while also keeping your options open longer.

In "Debriefing Chris Argyris: Combating Defensive Reasoning," Lauren Keller Johnson distills this Harvard Business School professor emeritus's insights about how effective communication can help you make savvy decisions. Too many managers, Argyris maintains, make poor choices or avoid making a decision at all because they're worried about embarrassing themselves, their boss or peers, or their organization. One way to avoid this mistake is to balance inquiry with advocacy when exploring others' responses to a decision you're considering. For example, "Here's why I think developing this new market makes sense. What do you think of my reasoning? Am I missing something you're seeing? And tell me more about what's making you lean toward exploring another market instead."

The last article in this section, Loren Gary's "Better Decisions? Keep Your 'Lizard Brain' in Check," offers an additional five tactics for strengthening your skills. 1) If you're facing a simple decision, imagine you've got just a few minutes to determine your course of action. For more complicated decisions, give yourself more time. 2) Assess how your decision will affect operations, productivity, and other aspects of your business. 3) If you feel paralyzed by the decision process, seek out a trusted colleague and talk things over. 4) Stop deliberating and make a decision if your best choices would disappear if you deliberated much longer. 5) When facing a bewildering number of decisions at one time, get started on the few that everyone around you agrees are the highest priorities.

Combating Cognitive Biases

All managers can fall prey to cognitive biases—errors in the thinking process—while making decisions. The articles in this section identify common types of biases and provide recommendations for recognizing and avoiding them.

Loren Gary starts the section with "Cognitive Bias: Systematic Errors in Decision Making." He introduces several typical biases and offers ideas for countering them. For example, in making decisions, we're often most influenced by information that is vivid, recent, and easily retrievable. Thus we may make the wrong choice because we've ignored other, equally relevant information. The remedy for this particular bias? Ask yourself whether you're considering the full range of information while considering your options. We also tend to seek information that confirms a decision we've already made—which can lead us equally astray. Instead, actively search for data that *dis*confirms your conclusion. That way, you'll know you're considering all possible angles.

In "Cognitive Bias in Everyday Strategic Planning," Gary shows how cognitive biases can come into play when managers are making weighty business decisions. For example, managers considering forging a strategic alliance often fall victim to the "availability heuristic"— the assumption that the most readily available information is the most pertinent. So they look to the most recent strategic alliance they made, and assume that the structure they selected for that arrangement is the same structure they should use for the next alliance. But strategic alliances can range in complexity from simple comarketing agreements all the way to a sharing of employees. Thus the structure of the most recent alliance may not be at all appropriate for subsequent alliances.

Journalist John Hintze introduces additional types of bias in "Why Do We Make Bad Decisions?" For instance, once we make an active, public commitment to a course of action, we tend to see that choice as more worthwhile than we did immediately before we made the decision. As a result, we close ourselves off from information that suggests our choice may not be the best. To guard against this and other types of bias, routinely audit your decision-making processes against a checklist of common snafus. Develop countermeasures that boost your ability to engage in independent thinking. For example, promise yourself that once you've committed to a course of action, you'll "sleep on it" for a few days to see if you still feel the same way about it later.

In this section's final article, "How Good Data Leads to Bad Decisions," business writer David Stauffer shines the spotlight on one particularly troublesome cognitive bias: the tendency to rely too much on historical precedent while making decisions. To combat this form of bias, consider these tactics: 1) Cross-examine every precedent you're considering, asking how relevant it is to the decision at hand. 2) If the historical precedent you're considering is so widely accepted in your organization that it's no longer challenged, research it to see whether it's as relevant as you think it is. 3) Encourage others to challenge your thinking about particular historical precedents. 4) Never rely solely on precedent to make a decision. 5) Develop a disciplined process for assessing precedents' relevance and moving decisions forward.

Leveraging Your Intuition

Intuition—the ability to know something without knowing *how* you know it—can help you improve the quality
of your decisions. However, that's possible only if you
take steps to improve your intuition's reliability, as well
as augment it with objective data while making decisions.

David Stauffer examines these practices in detail in
"Your Managerial Intuition: How Much Should You
Trust It?" According to Stauffer, intuition plays a larger
role in business decisions than ever before. Why? The
brisk pace of change and the possibility of missing out
on fleeting opportunities allow managers scant time for
leisurely analysis of their options. Using your intuition
can help you tackle time-sensitive decisions when you
have inadequate information at hand. Yet intuition is
most useful when you have expertise in particular areas.
For this reason, it's vital to build your expertise by gaining ever more experience in a given field. In addition,
open yourself to intuitive "flashes" by removing distractions and getting comfortable. Keep a diary to record
your state of mind when you have intuitive thoughts.
Over time, your diary can help you sort out intuitive
thinking from thoughts based merely on worries or
fears. Finally, test your intuitive feelings by discussing
options and preferences with an unbiased adviser or
friend.

In the closing article, "Decisions Don't Wait," Intel chairman and co-founder Andrew Grove shares his thoughts about intuitive decision making with Harvard Business School professor Clayton Christensen and business editor Walter Kiechel. According to Grove, too many managers exalt the virtues of data-driven decision making, at the expense of intuitive choices. Grove maintains that intuition can help you figure out "what to do"—while data can enable you to determine "how to do it well." Thus both intuition and data are essential. He also affirms that the more competent and knowledgeable you are about your business, the more confidence you can have in your intuition.

*   *   *

Making smart decisions will always be difficult. But by applying the practices and using the tools provided in this volume, you can greatly enhance your odds of choosing well—and reaping important benefits for your firm. As you read the articles that follow, keep the following questions in mind:

- What processes do you generally use to make basic business decisions, manage projects, and make tough ethical calls? If you're not satisfied with the quality of your decisions, what steps might you take to improve the processes you use?

- How do you allocate decision rights in your group? Do decision "owners" have sufficient information to carry out this important responsibility? If not, what changes might you make to your decision-rights allocation?

- While making a decision, what do you do to expand your "pool" of alternatives as much as possible? How might you improve this skill?

- How do you gauge the risks inherent in options you're weighing for a particular decision? Do you include strategic risks—such as changing customer preferences, the emergence of a one-of-a-kind rival, radical new technologies, and potentially fatal missteps?

- Do you gather a broad enough sampling of data, as well as input from stakeholders, while making a decision? If not, how might you do a better job of applying these practices?

- What cognitive biases tend to trip you up most frequently? What steps could you take to avoid falling prey to these biases?

- How often do you use your intuition while making decisions? What might you do to make your intuition as reliable as possible?

Using the Right Decision-Making Process

. . .

Everyone agrees that approaching decision making with a disciplined, clear process is valuable. But how do you choose from among the many established processes available? The following articles describe a number of processes that have been developed specifically for the managerial challenges you can expect to encounter.

You'll find a process for making basic business decisions, for selecting the right alternative when approaching a project milestone, and for making a tough call that has serious ethical considerations. You'll also discover a process for allocating decision rights—which determine who has the authority to make what types of decisions in your group, unit, or company.

Problem Solving for Decision Makers

• • •

Loren Gary

Suppose you're a brand manager in your company's gourmet snack foods division. After a number of successful years on the market, your sesame snack product has matured, and sales have begun to soften. A brand extension has been proposed. How do you decide if this is the right course of action?

Or perhaps you work for a computer superstore chain that wants to expand. You've been assigned the task of choosing where to locate new stores. Your team is generating lots of ideas for sites. How do you know when to call a halt to the research and select from among the various alternatives?

These situations underscore the extent to which solving problems is central to the work of the manager. And in the age of teams, managers don't solve problems alone. They must operate from a business discipline that will enable a group of workers to frame a problem and agree on the most efficient way to solve it. Yet as basic as this task is, many organizations don't solve problems using processes that result in optimal solutions. The signs of this are too much with us, from the frequent fizzling of comprehensive change-management efforts, to the stalling of "solutions" to more routine, circumscribed business problems such as the creation and marketing of new products and the expansion of a brand franchise or business.

Deficits in basic thinking skills are, in fact, felt at all levels of organizations. Chrysler, for example, has begun screening applicants for assembly-line jobs to see if they can demonstrate problem-solving skills. In the schools, the question "Why can't Johnny think?" has been added to the question "Why can't Johnny read?" Universities have been designing curricula to teach both basic and so-called higher-order thinking. At the Cognitive Research Trust Thinking Program, the basic approach is to identify simple procedures that can be applied to any problem. At Sonoma State University's Center for Critical Thinking, teachers are trained to model such competencies as clarity, precision, accuracy, relevance, consistency, and depth because the university believes students must work with others who can model such skills in order to learn them.

But companies can't wait for such reforms in education to percolate down into their work force. So what follows is a six-step guide for making basic business decisions, and some insights from a top tackler of management problems, General Electric.

The six-step model is taken from *Judgment in Managerial Decision Making* by Max Bazerman, J. Jay Gerber Distinguished Professor of Dispute Resolution and Organi-

> **Taking care to define the problem helps lead to optimal solutions.**

zation at Northwestern's Kellogg Graduate School of Management. It is a "prescriptive" model in the sense that it lays out an optimal approach to making decisions in a fully rational manner. Of course, real-world decision making regularly falls short of this purely rational ideal. But given the fog that can cloud critical thinking and problem solving in the workplace, a refresher on (or introduction to) some ideal problem-solving methods can only help. If nothing else, says Bazerman, "A good prescriptive approach helps you make sure you're asking the right questions."

Define the problem.

Defining, or framing, the problem is perhaps the most important step—if for no other reason than it's where most managers and teams first go astray. "We know less about problem definition than we do about decision-making errors and biases," acknowledges Bazerman. Nevertheless, there are some obvious mistakes that can be identified. For instance, defining the problem in terms of a proposed solution. In the gourmet brand example, focusing too quickly on the proposed brand extension can interfere with a more fundamental and broad-based analysis of the factors contributing to the brand's current health. Another example: diagnosing the problem in terms of its symptoms. Prematurely addressing the symptom of sluggish brand sales can lead to a misguided attempt to launch a new ad campaign. If the symptom is actually being caused by distribution snarls, those advertising dollars will be wasted. "So often we simply respond to the problems that come to us, when they aren't the right problems to be focusing on," cautions Bazerman. So don't let the symptoms or the proposed solution impede your effort to uncover the underlying problem.

Identify the criteria.

Most managers need to accomplish more than one objective when making a decision. In the computer superstore situation, the choice of new store locations will depend upon such factors as cheap commercial rental space, the existence of an adequately trained labor pool, proximity to existing distribution centers, ease of access for customers, and market research about sales potential in a given city or neighborhood.

Weight the criteria.

The relevant criteria will vary in importance, so once they have all been identified, they should be weighted— assigned a numerical value according to their relative importance. In the above example, if sales forecasts and rental costs are deemed five times more important than proximity to an existing distribution center, these differentials should be quantified by the numerical weight assigned to each criterion.

Generate alternatives.

"An inappropriate amount of search time is often spent seeking alternatives," writes Bazerman. "An optimal search continues only until the cost of search outweighs the value of the added information." Sometimes, of course, you can't know the value of the added information until after the fact; that is, until after it's been collected and analyzed. Still, your search for alternatives should be guided by the relative weights you've assigned to the relevant criteria. Returning to the superstore location, for example, allocate your time so that you're concentrating on alternatives that maximize sales potential and minimize rental costs.

Rate each alternative on each criterion.

Determining how well each alternative solution satisfies each of the identified criteria usually involves forecasting future conditions, never an easy prospect. But in this purely rational model, the potential consequences of choosing each possible alternative are carefully assessed and assigned a numerical value.

Compute the optimal decision.

If the first five steps have been done right, this last one is a straightforward matter. For each alternative, multiply the expected effectiveness of the alternative for each criterion by the weight assigned to each criterion. Adding up the totals for each criterion yields an overall score for the alternative. The alternative with the highest score is the rational choice.

Problem Solving for Teams

We've described a six-step model for individual decision making, but it's perfectly appropriate for teams as well, notes Bazerman, with some modifications. For example, he explains, "In a group setting you often have multiple definitions of the problem. Even though it may require spending more time on this step, it's important to agree on the problem definition before trying to generate alternatives." Moreover, a political dimension enters into the team context in a much more forceful way: Skillful political operators often try to manipulate the agenda by the way they frame a problem. Weighing the evidence for a particular problem definition—assessing it in light of the perspective of and potential benefit to the person offering the definition—thus takes on added importance.

Implementation and evaluation procedures become more crucial in a team context as well. "All the problem-solving approaches we use end up with these two components," says Steve Mercer, manager of executive education at General Electric's offices in Crotonville, New York. He outlines one approach that includes defining the problem, initiating immediate action to contain the problem (or minimize its harm) while its causes are being studied, verifying the cause of the problem, verifying the corrective action necessary, implementing the corrective action, and then doubling back to ensure that the problem doesn't occur again.

GE is adamantly opposed to the notion that one approach to problem solving will fit all situations, Mercer says. "At the corporate level, we try to avoid edicting processes to our constituent businesses, because then you create clones. A process that works for one of our manufacturing businesses may not be the best one for GE Capital. So we may expose people to five or six different approaches to problem solving in our executive education classes, but we don't promote any one particular model. Rather, we delegate the problem-solving courses to the training and development departments of the respective businesses. We tell each department to come up with the processes that make the most sense for its business."

In the real world of managerial decision making, where (research indicates) the average manager engages in a different activity every nine minutes, managers seldom have the luxury of the time it takes for such careful processes. Nobel laureate Herbert Simon has shown that in such settings purely rational judgment is "bounded" by time and cost constraints that limit the quality and quantity of available information, and also by the misperceptions and motivational biases to which decision makers fall prey. In other words, instead of making the optimal decisions prescribed by the rational model, managers "satisfice." As Bazerman writes, "They search until they find a solution that meets a certain acceptable level of performance."

In the real world, managers must make decisions amid uncertainty and the ever-pressing demands of time and tasks. The purely rational, prescriptive approach to decision making outlined here can, however, provide a framework for understanding how judgment can be optimized, when we have the will, and the time.

For Further Reading

Judgment in Managerial Decision Making by Max Bazerman (4th ed., 1998, John Wiley & Sons)

Reprint U9712C

Putting Real Options to Work to Improve Project Planning

• • •

Fabian D'Souza

For more than a decade, consultants and academics have been touting real options valuation (ROV) as a means of improving the decision making that goes into a project. To date, however, ROV has not been widely adopted as a planning tool. Many project managers worry that the esoteric Black-Scholes equations frequently used to evaluate real options would require the addition of expensive software and a specially trained finance expert to the project team.

But Black-Scholes is not the only valuation tool available. The familiar decision-tree framework is well suited to many of the contingencies that arise over the course of a project. When used as a strategic planning tool, decision analysis can help managers address issues such as how to allocate resources to ensure that the project meets specific deadlines, when to scale up or delay investments, and when to exit a project.

Matching the Tool to the Level and Type of Uncertainty

Much like a stock option, which gives the holder the right to purchase stock at a future date or at a set price, a real option gives managers a set of choices about capital investment that can be made as business conditions evolve. Think of it as a road map that optimizes decision making by enabling you to take multiple contingencies into account, plan your responses to them as they unfold, and phase your investments accordingly. When compared to net present value (NPV), the traditional formula for analyzing financial decisions, ROV has obvious advantages.

NPV assumes conditions of low uncertainty: the market conditions are known, the costs to completion of the project are predictable, the technologies involved are reliable, and the odds of winning any necessary regulatory approval are favorable. Whatever uncertainty exists is not enough for managers to contemplate changing the strategic plan in response to any of the outcomes. Opportunities are evaluated based on current information, and the NPV calculation of the projected cash flow of the investment under consideration results in one of two choices: go or no-go.

Most business decisions, however, are not of the now-or-never variety. Rather, their strategic plans change in accordance with the magnitude of the uncertainty. By assigning a quantifiable value to uncertainty, ROV enables decision makers to gauge and react to risk over time—quite a boon in a world besieged by constant price shifts, fluctuating interest rates, fickle consumer tastes, and emerging technologies.

Is the nature of the project you're managing such that you can alter your investment or resource-allocation decisions as the uncertainty is revealed or resolved? If you can, then ROV can play a valuable role in developing a strategic map to guide you through the decision-making process. A second question helps you determine the appropriateness of the decision-tree approach to ROV: is the uncertainty occasional or ongoing? In some arenas—energy and currency markets, for example—volatility is high and the future unfolds as an almost infinite number of possible outcomes. In most service industries and R&D–intensive industries, however, the uncertainties related to the management of a project tend to be milestone-driven. They arise as a result of a series of discrete choices presented under a limited number of scenarios; the decision-tree framework is best suited to such uncertainties.

Increasing Value through Project Redesign

A simple decision such as whether to develop a new technology in-house or acquire it from an outside party illustrates the utility of the decision-tree framework. In-house development requires three years and leads to three possible outcomes. In two of these outcomes, the firm expects to create significant value. But there's also a 25% chance that the in-house development would fail; obviously, this outcome would have no payoff. Figure 1 shows this decision using a decision-tree framework. The probabilities of the three outcomes are based on a combination of managers' experience and judgment.

After calculating the value of each alternative, the manager is able to pick the highest-valued alternative. For the acquisition alternative, subtracting the $10 million cost of acquisition from the $20 million payoff yields a value of $10 million. For each of the three outcomes in the in-house development alternative, you have to subtract the cost from the payoff and then multiply the result by the probability of success. Thus, for the

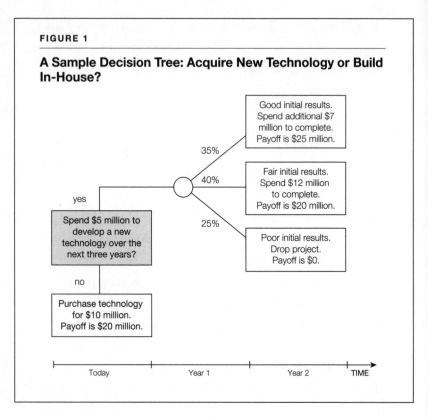

FIGURE 1

A Sample Decision Tree: Acquire New Technology or Build In-House?

most successful of the three outcomes, the expected value would be:

($25 million – $7 million) × .35 =
$6.3 million

An expected value calculation—the weighted average of the outcomes, with the probabilities used as weights— is used to blend the value of the three outcomes into a single number. A 10% cost of capital is used as the discount rate. Performing this calculation reveals the value of the in-house alternative to be $7.14 million, or less than 75% of the value of acquiring the technology from outside.

The decision-tree framework is useful not only for "organizing multistage projects that are subject to uncertainty," it can also help you redesign projects "for even higher value," writes management consultant Martha Amram in her book *Value Sweep*. Let's say that a manufacturing company is considering a $20 million investment to upgrade its existing plant so that it can introduce a new product line. This investment requires an additional $16 million in market research. If the research yields positive results, the company will proceed to launch the new product line. That launch is valued at $94 million (based on a discounted cash flow calculation). Both the infrastructure investment and the market acceptance have uncertain outcomes; those probabilities and a decision-tree diagram of the decision are shown in the top half of Figure 2.

Doing the calculations yields a negative NPV of $3.3 million for the project according to this initial design, which means that it's not worth doing. Another option is to redesign the project by running a smaller pilot market test while the infrastructure is being developed. Results from this pilot will help to resolve some of the market risk before the next decision point. If the infrastructure is successfully deployed, and the subsequent, comprehensive market research is successful, the project can move to product launch, saving time and money

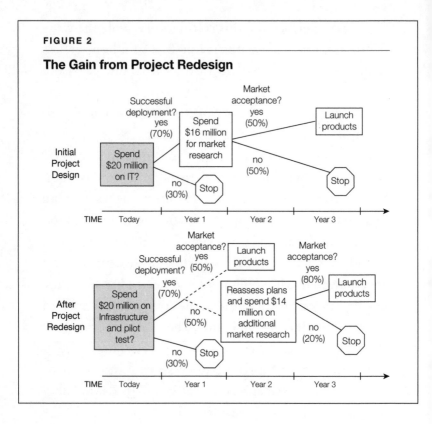

FIGURE 2

The Gain from Project Redesign

over the initial project design. The bottom half of Figure 2 shows a decision-tree diagram of the project after it has been redesigned along these lines.

The redesign enables the value of the launch and revised marketing plan to be folded back into the initial investment decision. The result, when you do the calculations, is an increase in the value of the project from a negative $3.3 million to a positive $5.5 million. In addition, with the redesign there is only a 37% chance that the project will be terminated, whereas the original design had a 65% chance of being scrapped.

Redesigning the project enables managers to learn more about the market at an earlier stage, thereby creating an opportunity to modify the marketing plan and increase the chance of market success. Under the revised plan, the project value increases because the follow-on investment is determined *after* some of the uncertainty has been resolved. The beauty of this decision-tree approach to ROV, therefore, is that it takes advantage of risk and uncertainty by tying expenditures more closely to the maturation of the opportunity. Breaking up the one market-research investment bet into two smaller investment bets enables the project manager to use options to improve his allocation of resources to the project as new information becomes available.

Process Concerns

Decision analysis is not without its implementation problems. For example, it can be difficult to get the relevant scientific and technical personnel to agree on the probabilities of failure or success for each stage of the project. In particular, managers who are invested in the success of the project often believe that the probability of success is close to 100%. Moreover, when a project is up and running, teams are frequently unwilling to discuss potential exit scenarios. This problem is particularly acute when managers have incentives to meet deadlines and milestones at any cost. The result is that midstream discussions about project closure are often biased.

To avoid these difficulties, make sure that you involve both business managers and technical personnel in creating the decision-tree diagrams. This will improve the buy-in that the project receives from both groups and will also make it easier to discuss plans for exiting the project if the outcomes are unsuccessful. Make sure that the two groups' incentives are aligned so that they are jointly accountable for the profitability of the project and the overall ROI of the portfolio of projects under way in your group. For instance, by giving rewards to project members for killing unsuccessful projects sooner rather than later, you increase the likelihood that even team members who have a strong personal investment in a particular project will agree to pull the plug if it's failing.

With these structural fixes in place, you're much better positioned to reap the chief benefit of the decision-tree approach to ROV: the improved coordination of spending with the potential outcomes of active learning.

For Further Reading

Value Sweep: Mapping Growth Opportunities Across Assets by Martha Amram (2002, Harvard Business School Press)

Reprint U0208C

How to Make Tough Ethical Calls

• • •

Jeffrey L. Seglin

In business, as in all things, the difference between right and wrong sometimes doesn't exist. It's often a matter of making the best "right" choice from several options. Making the best decision possible therefore requires rigorous and broad-minded thinking.

In an article I wrote for *Inc.* several years ago, I posed a dilemma, based on a real situation, that got at the heart of how tough making ethical decisions in business can be. A CEO of a $20 million company that repaired aircraft engines received a fax from an airline telling him that eight jets for which his company had repaired engine parts had been grounded because the turbines no longer functioned. The airline was claiming that this CEO's company's parts had caused the problem. Within an hour, he got another call telling him another aircraft had been grounded for the same reason. An hour later, another call came in. In all, 11 planes were grounded because of what the airline claimed were problems with his company's parts.

By the time the CEO received the first fax, the Federal Aviation Administration (FAA) had already been notified. So far, though, the FAA had not stepped in to shut his company down. And, remarkably, his company's name had managed to stay out of the press. If word got out and reached his lenders, the CEO feared they might pull his loans, which equaled his equity in the business.

> There are plenty of exercises designed to help you make the right call.

But since the FAA had begun an investigation, he reasoned that there was nothing to do but to sit tight until more details were revealed.

But as timing would have it, the company was in the midst of its annual audit. As part of the audit process, the CEO and CFO had to sign a letter assuring the auditors that they were informed of any outstanding circumstances that more than likely could have a negative financial impact on the company.

Coming clean on the audit statement might result in the financial demise of his company. "In my industry, there's a very tight code of ethics about the use of drugs or alcohol by a manufacturer's employees," the CEO said. "But there's nothing that tells you how you're supposed to deal with reporting information like this."

So here he was about to sign audit papers while trying to decide whether he was obligated to disclose the information about the failed engines despite the fact that he didn't yet have all the information on exactly what had happened. What should he have done? Disclose the information and risk the livelihood of hundreds of employees and his own stake in the company? Or stay mum until more information was available?

This is a tough one, as reader responses to the article confirmed. But while few of us will face a situation on such a grand scale, it's indicative of the decisions managers must make that have ethical implications, whether it's accepting basketball tickets from a vendor, withholding relevant information when giving a reference, or deciding whether to tell an employee asking you for financial advice that he's about to be laid off.

But there are plenty of exercises designed to help you make the right call. Peter Drucker recommends the "mirror test"—that is, asking, "What kind of person do I want to see when I shave . . . or put on my lipstick in the morning?" Norman Augustine, former CEO of Lockheed Martin, suggests four questions to ask yourself to help determine a course of action: (1) Is it legal? (2) If someone else did it to you, would you think it was fair? (3) Would you be content if it appeared on the front page of your hometown newspaper? (4) Would you like your mother to see you do it? "If you can answer 'yes' to all four questions," says Augustine, "then whatever you are about to do is probably ethical."

In his book *The Responsible Manager: Practical Strategies for Ethical Decision Making*, Michael Rion, an ethics consultant and former director of corporate responsibility for Cummins Engine Company, lays out a six-question guideline for ethical decision making. Looking at how the decision made by the CEO who faced the engine dilemma fits into this framework is instructive:

1. WHY IS THIS BOTHERING ME? The CEO is clearly concerned that disclosing the information will have a devastating effect on his company if word gets out.

2. WHO ELSE MATTERS? If word does get out, the employees may lose their jobs and the company's investors their invested capital.

3. IS IT MY RESPONSIBILITY? In answering this question, the CEO could look to the FAA investigation

and decide it's the FAA's responsibility to determine what happened.

4. WHAT IS THE ETHICAL CONCERN? From a legal perspective, the CEO figured he had to let the FAA know what happened, and it already knew. In terms of fairness and doing harm, the CEO's main concern was ensuring that neither his company nor his employees' jobs were destroyed by something that might turn out not to have been the result of his company's work.

5. WHAT DO OTHERS THINK? The CEO turned to his lawyers and his board for advice.

6. AM I BEING TRUE TO MYSELF? This is in line with the mirror test Drucker talks about. "What do I know about engines?" the CEO asked. "As a businessman, I was looking at this in terms of my survival."

Ultimately, the CEO decided not to disclose the information and signed the audit papers. The FAA eventually found it impossible to determine who was at fault for the engine failures. His company's name was never disclosed publicly as being a possible factor in the groundings.

These exercises can be helpful, but as you can see from the above example, they're ultimately only as good as the

The Sleep Test

One commonly accepted way to gauge if you've made the right decision in the face of an ethical dilemma is whether you can sleep at night. But as Joseph Badaracco Jr. points out in his book *Defining Moments: When Managers Must Choose Between Right and Right,* "people sometimes lie awake at night *precisely because they have done the right thing.* They understand that their decisions have real consequences, that success is not guaranteed, and that they will be held accountable for their decisions. . . . In short, if people like Hitler sometimes sleep well and people like Mother Teresa sometimes sleep badly, we can place little faith in simple sleep-test ethics."

people using them. What's missing, for example, in the CEO's response to "Who else matters?" is his concern for the safety of the passengers on the aircraft that used his company's engine parts. Years after the incident, the CEO acknowledged that the passengers' safety never crossed his mind when making his decision. It should have.

And it likely would have if the CEO had taken better measure of his impending decision's external effects. You can think of these effects as falling into three spheres: (1) money, meaning decisions involving capital and finance; (2) people—anybody the company works with, employs, or sells to; and (3) the community at large, the environment, or other bystanders. The goal is to assess how your potential actions will affect each of these spheres.

In the money sphere, the CEO considered that his bankers might call their loans and his investors might lose their equity if word got out. In the people sphere, he expressed concern over what impact disclosure would have on his employees' livelihood; if the banks started pulling loans, the company would have to downsize or shut down altogether. Where this CEO failed to assess the ethics of his decision was in the common-good sphere. He failed to question whether he had a responsibility to the passengers regarding the incident so they could make a decision about their own safety. After weighing this question, the CEO might still have signed the audit papers, calculating that it would be irresponsible to cause panic among passengers before more facts were known. The fact that he didn't ask the question showed a severe lapse in ethical reasoning.

So what is the "right" decision when it comes to signing the audit papers? There isn't one. Neither this nor any other process will provide a one-and-only solution. Different owners or managers facing similar situations could have responded in many ways, depending on the circumstances. And the response to the article from readers ranged from moral outrage at the CEO for being so reckless in his disregard for passengers to bafflement over why anyone would have decided not to sign the audit papers when full information wasn't yet known.

While there is no one "right" answer, going through the process ensures that you've conscientiously examined the effects your decision might have on the relevant constituencies. At some point, you have to make the decision; after all, you've got a business to run. But it's better to run it having weighed the impact your actions will have on the world in which you're operating.

Reprint U0504C

Put the Right Decisions in the Right Hands

· · ·

Peter Jacobs

How a company decides who is authorized to make what types of decisions can have a profound effect on its business, both in terms of everyday effectiveness and the bottom line.

Consider the experience of one global conglomerate that recently shifted to its U.S. headquarters final decision authority for the pricing of bids made by its foreign subsidiaries. The company believed that its U.S.-based executives would be more effective in making pricing decisions because they had a broader purview of the company's needs. But the time needed to transfer the relevant information to headquarters, and for executives there to absorb and react to it, reduced the company's ability to respond to bid requests on a timely basis. Alert to this change, a European rival added a 24-hour limit to its competing bids, forcing quick decisions from clients—and winning new business as a result.

Such a scenario "happens all too often," says Michael Jensen, professor emeritus at Harvard Business School and managing director of Monitor Group's organizational strategy practice. "Allocating decision rights in ways that maximize organizational performance is an extraordinarily difficult and controversial management task."

And therein lies a big problem, because how effective an organization is at making high-quality decisions consistent with its mission and objectives, the experts note, is a prime determinant of its ability to compete in the marketplace.

To better understand how the distribution of decision rights drives performance and what companies can do to allocate them more effectively, we spoke with several leading authorities and practitioners. We found that while the barriers to effective decision-rights distribution can be high, several best practices promise to lower them.

There are two types of costs that must be considered in allocating decision rights. In their 1990 paper, "Specific and General Knowledge, and Organizational

Avoid the Org-Chart Trap

Organization charts oversimplify the distribution of decision responsibility, say Michael Jensen and Keith Leslie. They make it much too easy to drop people into neat, interconnected boxes and to shift those boxes around with too little thought about the often-far-reaching consequences. Carl Spetzler, cofounder and chairman of Strategic Decisions Group, says, "I've seen many companies become dysfunctional by paying too much attention to their org charts and too little to the quality of decision making." Spetzler counsels clients to avoid thinking too much about decision "rights" and org charts because these emphasize power and judgment rather than decision quality.

Another problem with charts, he believes, is the mindset they create—one in which subordinates present supervisors with recommendations, and supervisors simply approve or reject whatever is presented. In this case, subordinates effectively become decision makers by choosing which alternatives to present. Though organization charts are helpful when creating operating efficiency and effectiveness, they are detrimental to cross-organizational strategic decisions.

Structure," in the *Journal of Applied Corporate Finance,* Jensen and the late William H. Meckling note these issues:

- The cost of delegating decision rights to those who have the relevant information but whose motivations and goals don't align with those of the company.

- The cost of accurately transferring the relevant information from the source to the decision maker.

Placing decision rights where these combined costs are minimal, the authors write, should lead to optimal decision-making efficiency and therefore better performance.

"If I know someone in the organization's lower levels can make a tough call that won't affect other parts of the company, then it's their call," says Nick Pudar, director of planning and strategic initiatives at General Motors.

But finding the organizational spot where decision costs are minimal is only part of the battle. You still must deal with the fact that those imbued with decision authority are invariably motivated by their own sets of personal and professional goals—some of which inevitably are inconsistent with those of the organization.

Overcoming these hurdles begins with the following steps.

1. Routinely review and update how decision authority is distributed

Because organizations, what they do, and the environment in which they operate continually change, decision-rights updates must become routine.

A review should examine carefully where in the organization various types of decisions are being made and whether those particular points are still the most efficient. Keith Leslie, a partner at McKinsey and Company's London office, says his firm recently advised one client to eliminate an entire management layer after such a review.

"Because they lacked sufficient information," he says, "these managers were making highly disruptive decisions about work allocation and subsequently had to spend much of their time quelling the resultant flare-ups. Those they managed were much better positioned to make such decisions themselves."

2. Avoid too much centralization—*and* too much democracy

Overcentralizing decision making is the biggest error companies make, Jensen says. Often as a leader, "you think you can make better calls," but decision rights must be collocated with the relevant information, and raising the level of decision-making authority thus requires transferring information upward as well. And

Metrics, Goals, and Incentives

When performance metrics align with organizational goals, better decision making results. This is particularly important when decision rights are widely allocated. For example, at Progressive Casualty Insurance Company, "We give product managers broad decision authority, then charge them with growing the business as fast as possible while achieving at least a designated level of underwriting profit," says Tom King, the company's treasurer. The product managers are then rewarded based on a combination of growth and profitability.

But not all companies achieve this level of clarity. "It's amazing how many companies I find rewarding employee actions that actually hurt their organizations and punishing those that help," says King. If, for example, your firm wants to bring in more midsized accounts and fewer large accounts, don't continue to reward your sales force based on total sales numbers; include a component that rewards them for bringing in accounts that fit optimally with the strategy.

companies often forget to do the latter or simply don't because the cost is too high.

You also need to avoid bringing too many people into the decision process, which can grind things to a halt. But be sure to involve all the key stakeholders.

To address these concerns, GM's Pudar employs an

innovative approach to consensus building. Prior to making major decisions about a new initiative, he says, "I meet individually with each group involved and ask three questions: 'What specific results will your organization deliver toward our goals?' 'What actions will you take to make it happen?' And, 'What do you expect other groups will contribute?' I then convene the group leaders and tell them all what they told me. The greatest differences are always their expectations of what other groups will do.

"While there has never been perfect alignment," he says, "this process enables us to rapidly identify and address the inconsistencies."

3. Assign decision rights unequivocally

Ambiguity about who has decision rights is a common problem. Misunderstandings about which individuals or groups have the right to make which decisions frequently carries a high cost for the organization, Jensen notes, whether through duplicated or counterproductive efforts, or through the failure of the parties to act.

Although this often is diagnosed as a communication breakdown, it's really a decision-rights assignment problem, says Jensen. Occasionally, managers forget entirely to inform those to whom they have given decision authority.

4. Don't confuse a particular outcome with the process itself

Good decisions occasionally produce bad outcomes. Kimberly Rucker, of TXU, says management is sometimes too quick to blame the decision makers or the process itself when results are not as expected. If decision rights are well allocated, then reallocating them because of a bad outcome will only make matters worse.

The experts agree that redistributing decision authority in any organization is a difficult task fraught with controversy and organizational politics. Yet, it is also one in which organizations must routinely engage to maintain a competitive edge and maximize shareholder value.

"As a company, we've recognized that good decisions don't just happen," says Rucker. "There is a science to it—a bit of art but a lot of science."

Reprint U0505B

Applying Potent Decision Tactics

* * *

Experts have developed numerous techniques for addressing specific challenges in decision making. In this section's articles, they share their advice. For example, you'll find helpful guidelines for expanding your "pool" of alternatives while making a decision. You'll also read about ways to assess the full range of risks associated with alternatives you're considering. An additional selection provides strategies for evaluating the information you gather while mulling over your options.

One expert even explains how to break a big, daunting decision into more manageable pieces. Another lays out a strategy for inviting stakeholders' input on a course of action you're proposing. The section closes with an article containing an additional five easy-to-remember tactics for strengthening your decision-making skills.

Debriefing Paul Nutt

Increase the Odds of Being Right

• • •

Lauren Keller Johnson

If you make decisions the way most people do, says Ohio State University management professor Paul Nutt, your decision is just as likely to be a failure as it is to be a success. And fifty-fifty is hardly a recipe for success in business.

By Nutt's definition, a failed decision is one that proves, for whatever reason, impossible to carry out. For example, you evaluate several new technologies for your unit, select one that you consider the most promising— and then promptly encounter stiff resistance from the people who will have to use it.

Failed decisions at any level in your company take a large toll in the form of wasted time, effort, and money. And poor decision making isn't limited to the inexperienced or intellectually inferior, says Nutt, author of *Why Decisions Fail: Avoiding the Blunders and Traps That Lead to Debacles.* "Even smart people in clever organizations make bad decisions," he says.

So what do you do? Learn to find the weak points in your decision-making processes, and move to eradicate them.

Taking Shortcuts: A Root Cause of Decision Failure

A major culprit behind failed decisions is a half-hearted search for alternatives during the decision-making process. Follow this approach, as most do, and you end up selecting from a limited pool of options, decreasing your odds of making the best possible decision.

We often feel compelled to "grab the first feasible choice that comes along, cram it down everyone else's throats, point to data that supports the choice, and then battle resistance when they try to implement it," Nutt says.

Why the rush to judgment and the stubborn clinging to one's ideas? Emotions—such as fear of being perceived as incompetent—play a large role.

"People in business are expected to succeed, and that's often defined as taking rapid, decisive action," Nutt says. "Impossible expectations are placed on people: they're being asked not to fail or make mistakes *and* to act rapidly. But what is the result of that kind of environment? They feel compelled to cover up their mistakes."

Though the pressure to engage in swift decision making may feel real to executives, "only one out of ten decisions really needs to be made quickly," Nutt says. "We usually have far more time to make a choice than we assume." Even in industries with fast product life cycles, such as the semiconductor sector, "the assumption that you *have* to make decisions instantly is invalid."

In addition to fear, "ego needs, a lust for power, and greed can tempt . . . decision makers to offer a self-serving idea . . . then move quickly to get endorsements for the idea," Nutt explains in a November 2004 *Academy of Management Executive* article.

Fear, greed, and power hunger aren't the only forces behind failed decisions. Cognitive limitations can also cause managers to take shortcuts when exploring alternatives. For example, a leader may assume that only the most influential stakeholders in a particular decision are able to offer worthwhile alternatives—so he ignores other stakeholders' valuable ideas and concerns. Or the decision maker falls into a kind of sunk-costs trap—becoming unwilling to pull the plug on a decision that she has advocated but that clearly isn't working.

Enlarging the Range of Possibilities

Expanding your pool of alternatives, Nutt argues, is one element of making smarter decisions. The more options you have to choose from, the more confident you can feel that you're making the optimal decision. But given the power of the emotions and cognitive limitations that can muddy decision makers' thinking, how can leaders resist the temptation to take shortcuts? It's difficult, acknowledges Nutt. But a few practices, systematically applied, can help.

Examine Your Motives

As you're considering alternatives before making a decision, step back and ask yourself if you're falling prey to the emotions and cognitive biases that typically derail decision makers.

"It's hard to be honest with yourself. You have to admit that you fear being seen as incompetent if you take more time to gather alternatives," Nutt says. "But awareness is half the battle."

For this reason, consider asking a coach or mentor to help you achieve the objectivity and distance you need to examine your motives honestly. A trusted friend or peer who has no stake in the decision at hand can also offer valuable perspective.

Finally, ask yourself how urgent your decision really is.

"With weighty decisions—such as whether to launch a new product line or which company to acquire—things usually aren't as urgent as they might seem," says Nutt. "You *can* take your time." And you should, given the huge volumes of information you typically will need to digest before committing to a choice.

Create a "Safe Space"

Many high-performing companies offer protected environments for managers to generate and explore decision alternatives. Nutt cites Disney's "dream room"—where people can freely brainstorm creative ideas without distractions and without fear of judgment or retribution—as a good example.

Obtaining a safe space to explore alternatives can be challenging, Nutt says, especially in organizations where creative people are viewed as impractical and flighty. "Many companies need a different culture entirely, one in which people are allowed to go into a contemplative mode for an hour." By modeling such behavior in your own organization or unit, you can help send the message that safe spaces matter.

Listen to More Stakeholders

Every decision has multiple stakeholders: people who have an interest in the decision's outcome or will be affected by it. You'll need their support to implement your decision. Ignore their ideas and concerns, and you risk catalyzing resistance when you try to put your decision into action.

Where should you look for stakeholders? Depending on the magnitude of your decision, Nutt suggests considering members of top-management teams, leaders of key departments, and technical experts. Individuals in your organization with relevant experiences, union members, suppliers, customers, and competitors can also constitute stakeholders. Finally, activist groups and

> Look for win-win alternatives that address overlapping concerns across many stakeholder groups.

members of the general public may be important stakeholders in politically sensitive, high-level decisions.

To assess the broadest possible stakeholder viewpoints, invite your stakeholders to participate in focus groups specifically aimed at exploring their concerns regarding the decision in question. This simple action enhances your credibility and begins mobilizing support behind your decision process. Look for potential win-win alternatives that address overlapping concerns across many stakeholder groups. Identify and consider the interests of stakeholders who might have the power to block your decision.

Set Broad Objectives for Your Decision

For each decision you're considering, define objectives that have multiple possible solutions. The more solutions you can generate, the more alternatives you have to choose from. According to Nutt, Shell Oil failed to do this when it adopted a deep-sea disposal plan for its Brent Spar oil-storage facility floating in the North Sea. Shell's primary objective for this decision was to minimize costs, which pointed to deep-sea disposal of the facility. A broader objective would have suggested more options, such as having interested parties debate what would be the best disposal approach.

By focusing on its narrow objective of cutting costs, Shell committed itself to the deep-sea disposal plan. But before it could carry out the disposal, environmental activists boarded the Spar and protested the action. The event—along with Shell's failed attempt to remove the activists with high-pressure hoses—earned the company lurid newspaper headlines and forced it to abandon the plan.

Study Past Decisions

Analyzing cases that document unsuccessful decisions can help some managers avoid making similar mistakes. But if you take this tack, Nutt warns, focus your effort on tracing what went wrong—not on deriding the hapless decision maker featured in the story.

Also study your own past decisions—unsuccessful *and* successful. Identify what went well and what didn't go well, and what you might do differently next time. Ask questions such as, "Where did I miss an opportunity to generate additional alternatives? At what point did I commit myself heart and soul to my choice—regardless of whether it was wise?"

"It's valuable to conduct a debrief after every decision," says Nutt. "And before making the next decision, develop a checklist of all the questions you need to ask and people you need to consult to generate the widest possible pool of alternatives."

Reprint U0506C

What Are the Risks You *Should* Be Taking?

* * *

Adrian Slywotzky

Most managers treat risk as an unwanted byproduct of the business—something to be controlled whenever possible. That way of thinking stems from an overly simplistic view of risk. Some risks should be minimized, but others should be embraced in the drive for growth.

Indeed, the pursuit of growth requires placing bets on specific products, customer segments, channels, company alliances, and so on—all of which entail management of *strategic* risk. The most successful companies do not try simply to defend against bad risk events; they also define and predict the upside risks that, when well managed, can deliver the maximum rewards.

Thinking About Risk

To exploit the benefits of risk, managers must first broaden the way they think about it. Most tend to think narrowly of financial, operating, and hazardous risks, such as currency fluctuations, fraud, and earthquakes. And their defense consists of practices aimed at mitigating or transferring risk, such as hedging, internal controls, and insurance.

But beyond these traditional risks, there is also a set of strategic risks that have become increasingly disruptive and a larger source of value destruction. Failure to anticipate and manage the spectrum of strategic risks can expose a company to dramatic drops in shareholder value as well as volatility in earnings. For example, the number of U.S. companies that are able to achieve long-term stable earnings growth has fallen, as reflected by the steady decline in the ratio of high-quality to low-quality Standard & Poor's stocks (with quality measured by earnings stability), from 66% in 1985 to 19% in 2003.

Strategic risks include more than the obvious, high-probability events that a new ad campaign or new-product launch will fail. Virtually every strategy shift—whether a modest or a major change in the business model—contains other less-obvious risks as well:

- Customers' priorities will change quickly, such as when parents migrated from station wagons to minivans, catching most automakers off guard.

- New technology will overtake your product, in the same way that mobile telephony stole market share from fixed-line voice.

- One misdeed will cause your brand to collapse, as befell Martha Stewart.

- A one-of-a-kind competitor will render your business model obsolete, such as the Wal-Mart tidal wave that washed over midrange department stores.

But there is an upside to risk as well. And without the willingness and capability to recognize and mine the rewards of strategic risk, companies place significant limits on the likelihood of success. Consider the array of countermeasures that address—even embrace—strategic risks.

Smart Sequencing for Growth Initiatives

In the mid-1990s, Cardinal Health was just one of several large competitors in the low- and declining-margin pharmaceutical distribution business. Looking for fresh avenues of growth, the company started to provide new offerings in immediately adjacent market spaces. First it entered a series of adjacent businesses, such as pharmacy management and automated drug dispensing in hospitals. When it succeeded in these areas, Cardinal added higher-value services in pharmacist staffing and consulting. For drugmakers, the company started with drug packaging and then moved into contract manufacturing and formulation.

Cardinal moved deliberately, leveraging its assets and customer relationships to gain the experience, knowledge, and reputation necessary to take the next step with confidence and its customers' trust. Smart sequencing into new, larger markets has made the company the undisputed industry leader in financial performance. By establishing itself carefully along specific points of the value chain, Cardinal spread its risks and was able to sustain growth.

Using Proprietary Information to Reduce the Risk of Each New Initiative

Johnson Controls' business was once based on commoditized products, such as car batteries and car-seat frames, so the company was vulnerable to intense price competition. But during the past 15 years, JCI has developed a broad range of assembly, integration, and R&D skills that distinguish it from the competition. The company now designs and assembles entire vehicle cockpits, and its Comfort Lab conducts more customer research on interiors than any automaker.

Because of its unique capabilities, JCI now has continual contact with one automaker's entire design and engineering team. The company's involvement spans the vehicle planning process, gathering and generating proprietary information that produces a depth of insight into the automaker's needs and activities that traditional parts suppliers cannot match. This makes JCI a supplier of choice, reducing bidding volatility and allowing it to plan with greater certainty. JCI's revenues, profits, and market capitalization have all shown a compound annual growth rate in the double digits for the past decade.

In the consumer world, where preferences can shift quickly and unexpectedly, Japanese video and music retailer Tsutaya conducts a continual analysis of customer spending patterns, using point-of-sale data, surveys, and databases. Tsutaya can pinpoint individual family or customer preferences, allowing it to anticipate the way tastes are changing. The company has significantly outgrown all of its competitors as a result of generating the best proprietary information in the industry, and it even sells its data to other companies seeking to track shifts in customer priorities better.

Double Betting to Minimize
the Risk of Obsolescence

When several versions of a new technology compete to become the standard, it's impossible to predict which will prevail. So smart managers make double bets. Betting on both Windows and OS/2 positioned Microsoft to win, no matter which operating system prevailed. Similarly, Intel's double bet on both RISC and CISC chip architecture ensured its success in semiconductor chips. Barnes & Noble, by contrast, failed to bet early enough or big enough on the Internet as a channel for book sales alongside its physical stores. That slow start gave Amazon the opening it needed to dominate book, and then online media, sales.

Shifting the Compete/Collaborate Ratio
to Avoid a No-Profit Zone

When an industry matures and offerings among various companies grow similar, the industry risks becoming a no-profit zone. The most effective proven countermeasure to industry economics risk is to increase collaboration among the relevant firms. Collaboration can take many forms, including sharing of back-office functions, asset-sharing or coproduction agreements, repair or maintenance collaboration, purchasing and supply-chain coordination, joint research and development, and collaborative marketing.

Most companies begin collaborating five to 10 years too late. When the industry is new and growing—and margins are fat—it can afford to support a compete/collaborate ratio of almost 100/0. The ratio begins to shift only when margins have eroded, as has happened with airlines, utilities, steel, computing, and memory chips. The challenge is to anticipate the threat and prepare for it by laying the groundwork for collaboration in advance.

Airbus is a notable exception to the "start too late" phenomenon. Declining industry economics in the early 1970s could not support many aircraft makers going it alone in Europe. They created a consortium that shared resources, eliminated redundancies, and enabled them to remain competitive.

Helping Customers Control
Their Own Risks

Coping with a car accident is the most time-consuming, hassle-filled experience associated with car ownership. Progressive Insurance has grown to be the third-largest U.S. auto insurer not because its coverage is different but because of the way it helps customers control the risks of increased anxiety and lost time.

Progressive has built a high-speed comprehensive

claims-management service, featuring a fleet of "immediate response vehicles" equipped with laptop computers, intelligent software, and wireless access to the firm's claims department. An assessor can arrive on the scene—often within an hour of the accident—ascertain the damage, approve the necessary repairs, and cut a check on the spot. And the insurance provider has recently taken its initiative a step further: in the spring of 2003, Progressive launched "one-stop" claims service centers that allow customers to manage the repair process themselves or allow a Progressive claim representative to do so. If customers choose the latter, they are free of many typical insurance hassles. Progressive has thrived by eliminating risks for the consumer.

Traditional risk management seeks to contain losses. But that's just half of the growth equation. By embracing strategic risk, Cardinal, JCI, Tsutaya, Progressive, and other risk-savvy companies have raised their growth potential while reducing their economic volatility.

Just as banks during the past 15 years have refined tools to manage credit risk, tools to address strategic risk are now becoming more readily available. Even traditionally soft areas such as branding can now be analyzed with rigor. Managers thus can pursue new growth more aggressively and more prudently.

Reprint U0410D

What Leaders Allow Themselves to Know

• • •

Paul Michelman

How could Julius Caesar have been blind to the warnings about his imminent fall even as they fell like hail upon him? Why didn't Compaq CEO Eckhard Pfeiffer listen to the senior managers who urged him time and again to pay attention to the upstart PC makers who were siphoning off Compaq's customers? How is it that former *New York Times* executive editor Howell Raines continued to engage in the very behaviors that had alienated an entire newsroom even after a 17,000-word article in the *New Yorker* made his problems as plain as a five-column headline?

According to leadership scholar Warren Bennis, to comprehend the curious actions—or inactions—taken by these leaders in the face of turbulence, we must first look at the way they dealt with the information available to them, specifically "what they allowed themselves to know and when they allowed themselves to know it."

Bennis, who is a Distinguished Professor of Business Administration at the University of Southern California and also holds advisory roles at Harvard Business School and Harvard's Kennedy School of Government, has been reshaping our perceptions of leadership for five decades. He sat down with *Harvard Management Update* to discuss his thinking about the way leaders process information. His ideas provide a framework for understanding decision making by looking at how and why our minds accept or reject certain information, particularly disconfirming information.

The Barriers to Better Decisions

We all employ filters, Bennis says, that direct the flow of information in our minds. These filters govern which data lands on the active agenda of our consciousness and which gets shuttled off to the mind's dark corners. "For a variety of reasons, the mind doesn't give you license to interpret certain data," he says. "You don't deal with the issues that you don't want to believe are real, and this leaves you with a skewed vision." Could that explain, Bennis asks, why the White House plowed ahead with making its case for war in Iraq when hindsight suggests officials should have seen that some data used to build the justification was not airtight? Did the president's passionate belief that the White House's plan was right for the country allow information that supported his preconceptions to trump disconfirming data?

> "The tragedy is how we lose good people because they cannot listen or don't want to listen."

If so, Bush's decision-making process illustrates one of the three filters Bennis has identified as governing the flow of data into the conscious mind: *social filters*. These are filters that allow leaders to reject certain data by simply not paying attention to its source. "When I was in Abu Dhabi a couple of years ago, a colleague there told me about a Middle Eastern phrase used in describing people who stop listening," Bennis says. "He called it 'tired ears.'"

Think about Pfeiffer, who led nearly seven years of uninterrupted growth at Compaq before things took a profound turn for the worse. "He had an A list and a B list," Bennis says. "And his A list said, 'Yes, sir,' 'Aye, aye, sir'" to whatever strategy Pfeiffer would proffer. "But the B list was saying, 'Hey, boss, you know maybe we better look at what Gateway's doing or what Dell is doing because they're taking away a lot of our customers.' Pfeiffer didn't listen to or look at the evidence. Eventually, he just stopped seeing the people on the B list who were giving him disconfirming, bad news. He had tired ears."

So did Pfeiffer deliberately put himself in a position in which certain information couldn't reach him because he wanted to avoid dealing with what he *knew* was true? Not necessarily, Bennis says. It's possible he simply began to ignore any data that did not affirm what he *believed,* on some level, to be true. It's important to distinguish that kind of blindness to information from the legal concept of *willful blindness,* in which an individual purposely closes himself off to data in order to create ignorance-by-design of certain facts—for instance, what former Enron CEO Kenneth Lay may have engaged in. The forces at work here are often of a less conscious and purposeful nature.

Look, too, Bennis says, at Shakespeare's Caesar. The evidence screams danger. "His wife dreams of him as a bleeding statue with 100 spouts and lusty Romans washing their hands in his blood. An owl hooted, which meant a lot in 44 B.C. Rome. A lion ran through the streets."

But Caesar ignored the signs at every turn. He wouldn't even accept the note warning about Cassius, Casca, and Brutus that Artemidorus tried repeatedly to give him. "Why is it that he didn't pay attention?" Bennis asks. The same question could be asked about Pfeiffer, Raines, and countless others who have encountered great leadership failures, he says. "The tragedy is how we lose good people because they cannot listen or don't want to listen."

If social filters allow us shut out particular sources of information, *contextual filters* let us reject the significance of our surroundings. To explain, Bennis turns to his own experiences as president of the University of Cincinnati from 1971 to 1978. "I was brought in to rattle the cages and to make that city-supported school into a major state university," he says. "Here I was, a kind of foreigner, and the people in Cincinnati thought I was stealing the university away from them." So the 80-something Fred Lazurus Jr., founder of Federated Department Stores, offered what Bennis describes as wise counsel. "He said, 'Warren, this is a real conservative city. Don't be too visible. Work with your faculty, work with your students. Don't get sucked into the limelight.'"

But Bennis didn't really try to understand the culture he was dealing with, and when his saber rattling at the university caught the attention of the press, he didn't exactly play the role of shrinking violet. *Cincinnati Magazine,* for instance, wrote a profile that made Bennis, his work, and his family "look like Camelot," he says. "I kind of enjoyed it." He was even talked into hosting a local television program called *Bennis!*

Not surprisingly, those highly visible trappings of leadership did not always sit well with the constituencies whose support Bennis's mission required, making his role as change agent all that more difficult.

"Here's the lesson about context," Bennis says. "I didn't take the time to understand the city—its pride, its history. I didn't take time to honor it."

Consider another leader brought in to effect change: Hewlett-Packard's Carly Fiorina. "There were three strikes against her to begin with," Bennis says. "She's a woman, not an engineer, and the first non-Hewlett-Packard person ever to be elevated to the top level. How does she navigate between the past and the present?"

What Fiorina has done is carefully use symbols of HP's rich tradition in spelling out her vision of the future. For example, she initially employed the image of Dave Packard and Bill Hewlett as the boys in the garage to create excitement for how HP would continue to generate groundbreaking ideas. The awareness of the situation that Fiorina displayed allowed her to remove the contextual filters that may have led her to a different, less effective approach to communicating her vision for HP.

The third and final filter that Bennis identifies is governed by *self-knowledge:* what you know and don't know about yourself. To explain, Bennis turns again to his own experience.

"For a lot of reasons, some having to do with ambition, some having to do with wanting to see whether my ideas really had validity on the ground, I had the desire to be a university president," Bennis says. "I wanted to be one so bad that I left my MIT job, where I had what every professor dreams of—a corner office, tenure at a great institution—and I took a job as provost at SUNY Buffalo." Four years in Buffalo then led to the opportunity that Bennis had been waiting for, a university presidency at Cincinnati.

After seven years at the helm of the university, Bennis delivered a speech at the Harvard Graduate School of Education on the leadership role of a university president. "I worked very hard on the talk, and I thought it went really well," he recalls. "And then I took Q&A."

From the back of the room, Paul Ylvisacker, then dean of Harvard's Graduate School of Education, floated what Bennis describes as "a real knuckleball" of a question: "'Warren, do you *love* being president of the University of Cincinnati? Do you love being president?' I was totally stumped. . . . But I finally was able to look up at him and say, 'Paul, I don't know.'"

Later, on the plane back to Cincinnati, Bennis realized "what it was that Paul was picking up in my eyes," he says. It was that Bennis's heart was not in being president—he just didn't have the passion. He realized later, he says, that being a university president was "not my calling."

As a result of Ylvisacker's question, Bennis was forced to confront his lack of self-knowledge and, in doing so,

> A lack of "self-knowledge is the most common, *everyday* source of leadership failures," Bennis says.

was able to make a decision that was very different from the one he had made a decade earlier. In effect, he had gained a greater level of control by opening up the filter governed by self-knowledge.

When leaders lack self-knowledge, Bennis says, their decision-making capabilities are compromised. No matter what information is available to you, if you don't know yourself—what drives you to do what you do—the likelihood of misinterpreting and misusing that data increases dramatically.

A lack of "self-knowledge is the most common, *everyday* source of leadership failures," Bennis says. "A lot of gifted individuals I've known over the years who found themselves leading organizations aspired to that top position without knowing what it entailed and what was in store for them. They wanted to *be* a CEO but didn't want to *do* a CEO's job. That's the first question I ask all 'high-potential' leaders. Do you know what's in store, and do you know if the role fits your skill set and/or your 'best self.' That's exactly what I didn't ask myself."

Pursuing the "Full Spectrum" of Data

Building a greater base of knowledge about one's circumstances is the critical element in eliminating the role of all three of the filters Bennis identifies. Harking back to the story of Caesar, Bennis wrote recently in his column for *CIO Insight* magazine, "Wise leaders know to beware not the ides of March, but the likelihood that their power will isolate them." They then take action to guard against that isolation, he says, both before and after making decisions. When Clark Clifford took over the Defense Department from Robert McNamara during the war in Vietnam, "he began talking to people at every level of the organization, not just the direct reports, not just getting the usual news," Bennis says. "FedEx CIO Robert Carter holds frequent town-hall meetings with his staff and cultivates candor by sharing a meal every month with eight employees," he writes.

Bennis urges leaders to take that strategy one step further by engaging in decision-making postmortems that give leadership teams the opportunity to revisit the reasoning behind a decision before a plan of action is implemented. After the members of the GE board had come to an agreement to name Jeff Immelt to succeed Jack Welch, for example, the board took three weeks—on Welch's recommendation—to let the decision sit before the official vote was taken and an announcement made.

Leaders must always be certain they are accessing the full spectrum of data and opinion, Bennis says. "I think the best leaders find out the way Henry V found out," he notes. On the eve of battle, "he took off his royal robes, put on an enlisted man's army clothes, and he went off and huddled with the troops and asked them what was going on."

Reprint U0402C

Put Your Decision Making to the Test

Communicate

• • •

Nick Morgan

Nick Leeson and Barings Bank have become, respectively, the poster child and poster company for bad decision making. You remember them—Nick Leeson was the trader whose attempts beginning in 1992 to cover up trading mistakes and losses mushroomed into a billion-dollar loss and the collapse of the bank.

How did it happen? Why didn't anyone in Singapore, where Leeson was based, stop him before the loss became catastrophic? Why did it take so long for HQ in London to respond to the crisis? The answers to these questions suggest the critical steps in a bad decision-making process—an object lesson in How Not to Do It—and point the way toward making better decisions. The bad news is that most of us make decisions just the way Leeson and Barings did—but we think we don't. The good news is that we can learn to make better ones.

Can you pass the "skeptical colleague" test?

The key lesson from the Barings fiasco is that business decisions—and even most personal ones—should never occur in a vacuum. You need to communicate, at some point to someone, the case for your important decisions. Indeed, the process itself, of developing the communications case, is the single best method for ensuring a good decision. If you can tell a convincing story that presents the basis for your decision to a skeptical colleague, explaining what it is and how you arrived at it, what the alternatives were and why you rejected them, then the chances are good that you've given your decision sufficient thought. Barings' top management made the fundamental mistakes first of hiring Leeson (with a flawed résumé) without sufficient discussion, and then of allowing Leeson to operate alone without sufficient safeguards. Leeson in his turn failed to communicate his mistakes early on, thus turning retrievable errors into calamity.

Stephen J. Hoch and Howard C. Kunreuther, professors at the Wharton School of Business and editors of *Wharton on Making Decisions,* identify several additional mistakes that Barings' managers made and to which we are all prone.

Bad decisions overrely on intuition and emotions.

"When Barings entered the futures business," Hoch and Kunreuther write, "it was essentially a one-man operation (Christopher Heath) that relied on an instinctive style of management. As business expanded rapidly, Heath and Barings failed to recognize that such an intuitive management style was no longer appropriate." Many businesses that grow rapidly develop managers that suffer from this kind of seat-of-the-pants decision making. They learned the business when one person could understand it all and make good decisions. Even after that changed, they still make decisions in the same way. What's needed instead is a mixed model of information systems and human intuition. In other words, when the decisions become complicated, set up good communications systems that allow for sufficient input.

Bad decisions underestimate risk.

As Hoch and Kunreuther say, "Decision makers have great difficulty in evaluating low-probability, high-risk events before disaster strikes, so they tend to underprotect themselves beforehand and overprotect themselves afterward."

We see this decision-making pattern playing out from one generation to the next. For example, Depression-era managers learned fiscal caution from the extreme conditions of the 1930s, while Boomer managers had no similar catastrophe to teach them viscerally about financial restraint in their own formative business years. Again, good decision makers adopt communications systems that allow for reality checks against their mental models, models that often are deeply embedded in their thought processes and therefore hard to recognize for what they are.

Bad decisions result from the need for speed.

"Barings executives also appeared to make decisions quickly," say Hoch and Kunreuther, "racing to take advantage of market opportunities and failing to institute a sufficiently rigorous system of controls. . . . This Westernized, time-is-money attitude contrasts with an Eastern view, which emphasizes patient reflection. . . . The expedient, time-is-money mode may not always lead to the very best choice, but there are times when speed is critical." The pace of decision making in the West has increased enormously in the Internet era, and we have even seen attempts to make a virtue out of the necessity of making fast decisions with incomplete information, as if that were somehow a good model. In fact, that model often leads to a higher ratio of bad decisions. Sometimes, however, there must be a tradeoff. Some decisions simply can't be delayed to wait for perfect information.

Let's say you've learned to avoid the traps that catch the unwary in the decision-making process. You've managed to look skeptically at your emotions, and you're using your intuition judiciously. More than that, you've learned to weigh risk and move when the time is right—not before. You regularly solicit outside input to your sense-making and data-gathering systems so that your decision making is based on strong communications processes that include facts and input from colleagues. What criteria do you use to make a great decision? Many of the decisions we make involve competing potential benefits—how do we decide amongst them?

In this happy situation, the experts advise, there are some rules that can guide you to great decision making. The first step is to figure out whether the decision you need to make is one you can make alone or one that necessarily involves others.

If you need others to implement a decision, involve them in the process.

"If people don't own the solution to the problems or agree to the decision, implementation will be half-hearted at best, probably misunderstood, and more likely than not, fail," says Michael Doyle, a pioneer in the field of participatory decision making.

Once you've figured out how many people need to be involved, you're ready to focus on the issue to be decided. Here, the experts advise setting clear criteria.

Focus on the most important criterion.

Says Charles Foster, director of the Chestnut Hill Institute, and author of *What Do I Do Now?: Dr. Foster's 30 Laws of Great Decision Making,* "The most important law for shining the biggest spotlight fastest on what's best for you to do is to *focus on the most important thing.*"

Some of the most difficult decisions involve both personal and business issues. While companies may have a series of decision-making checkpoints, the same systems usually don't exist for career moves. Most of us face decisions that overwhelm us with a surfeit of possible criteria. Say, for example, that you're trying to decide whether to move to a distant city to take advantage of a promotion. The promotion is in a new division, and it involves greater risk than the division you're in right now. It might fail, leaving you high and dry and a long way from home. Your kids are halfway through elementary school, and one of them has just settled down with a great teacher. Your spouse cannot easily replicate the job he has in the distant town.

You have too many criteria to make an effective go/no-go decision. So decide what the most important criterion is for you right now. Foster offers several criteria for how to pick that single most important criterion. First, he says, "It's something that will make your life wonderful . . . or it's something that will enable you to take care of your most important responsibility . . . or it's something that will make it possible for you to solve your biggest problem." Begin a dialogue with yourself—or with a friend or colleague—to help you develop the right kinds of feedback and self-knowledge.

> For better decision making, decide what the most important criterion is for you right now.

Then, using the example above, ask yourself, what's most important? Is it the children's schooling? Or taking that great new opportunity? You can't begin to make an effective decision until you rate the criteria you're considering. And how do you know if you're rating those criteria correctly? Foster says, the correct criteria are "more likely long-term than short-term . . . more to do with what you want than with what other people want, [and] . . . more likely connected to your hopes than your fears."

Once you figure out what the most important criterion

is, give it more weight than all the others. Communicate the logic of this new understanding to a friend or colleague in your confidence. See if you can convince that friend—and yourself—that what you're saying makes sense.

Consider the upside.

Far too many of us fall into damage-control mode when faced with a difficult decision. We forget to look at the upside—all the good things that might happen. Even if they are not likely to happen, they are important to the process, because of course they won't be realized if your decision is ultimately not to proceed. In the example above, you have no chance of realizing the rapid growth potential of the new business venture if you stay put.

Test your decision against the future.

In the same vein, Foster argues that "good decision makers are not blinded by the now. They take the present situation and play it out in their heads to see what happens to it over time."

In our hypothetical example, looking into the future might involve guessing whether or not the kids will adjust to a new school, and how well your spouse will do finding work in the new town.

Break big decisions down into a lot of little ones.

Often we feel overwhelmed by some huge decision like relocating, taking a new job, or the like. We tend to see it as an either-or fork in the road. Either you go one way or the other. And all too often, people linger at the fork, paralyzed by the fear of commitment to one irrevocable path or the other.

And yet, often the issue can be broken down into a series of small decisions with continuous feedback loops. Perhaps you can take a week's vacation and spend it in the new town, getting a feel for the area and researching the business climate. Small steps don't make the big one inevitable—you've kept your options open. And you've started to get a feel for what the move would be like.

Keep your options open.

Don't allow yourself to be rushed into a decision. Make the decision when you're ready, not when everyone else wants you to. Of course, there are times when events force a decision on you. Then, you want to keep your options open as much and as long as possible. As Foster says, "People who make bad choices not only end up in a worse place, they also find that they've made it harder for themselves to make good decisions in the future. That's because bad decisions bring you to a place where you have fewer, worse options."

Finally, don't decide unless you have to.

Peter Drucker, the management guru, says, "There is one final question the effective decision maker asks: Is a decision really necessary? *One* alternative is always the alternative of doing nothing. Every decision is like surgery. It is an intervention into a system and therefore carries with it the risk of shock. One does not make unnecessary decisions any more than a good surgeon does unnecessary surgery."

Reprint C0111A

Debriefing Chris Argyris

Combating Defensive Reasoning

• • •

Lauren Keller Johnson

What do Enron, the CIA, and the Catholic Church have in common? Leaders in these organizations committed egregious mistakes and cover-ups that stemmed from *defensive routines*—behaviors intended to prevent individuals, groups, or organizations from embarrassment or threats, says Chris Argyris, professor emeritus at Harvard University.

Leaders who practice defensive routines don't simply "spin" or hide the truth when it's potentially embarrassing or threatening; their defensive reasoning leads them to cover up the fact that they're covering up. Moreover, they discourage opposing viewpoints and blame others or "the system" for mistakes. As a result, errors in thinking go unexamined, and poor decisions go uncorrected.

Not all defensive reasoning leads to wholesale organizational failure, but the defensive routines it fosters stand in the way of effective communication and can render companies unable to learn and, thus, unable to improve.

Although eradicating defensive routines is difficult, their existence is so prevalent—and so damaging—that leaders have no choice but to try.

Understanding the Underground Organization

People at all levels in an organization use defensive routines, says Argyris, who is also a director emeritus of the consultancy Monitor Group, and the problem exists in every company and industry.

Defensive routines are not only widespread, they are frustratingly persistent and deeply ingrained. "We learn to create defensive routines early in our lives," Argyris says. "As adults, we help foster organizational climates that support those routines. The cycle becomes self-reinforcing."

The result? Defensive routines create a kind of underground organization in which people's behavior bears little relation to the aboveground organization—a company's stated values and ways of doing business. For instance, a CEO professes that he wants open and honest feedback on his leadership style from senior executives. But on several occasions, this same CEO acts upset or angry when an executive provides critical feedback. The executives respond by building up the underground organization: among themselves, they define and share

> Dead giveaways include "Trust me—I know how things work in this place."

"rules" for dealing with the CEO, such as "Sense his mood before you open your mouth," or "Remember: he'll blame us for his bad decisions."

So how can executives and managers root out defensive routines and replace them with more productive ones? A commitment to self-reflection is essential. The following practices will also help:

1. Know the symptoms

Defensive routines reveal themselves in several ways. For example, managers can detect them by listening carefully to how people in the organization craft arguments. "If others are presenting claims in ways that prevent you from testing their validity," Argyris says, "defensive thinking is going on." Although sometimes one needs to pay careful attention to hear clues of this kind of thinking, dead giveaways include comments such as "Trust me—I know how things work in this place," or "He'll never change."

2. Examine both unstated and stated thoughts and feelings

Argyris recommends an exercise he calls the Left-Hand/Right-Hand Columns, which can help managers surface defensiveness in their own thinking. To use this technique, a manager first divides a piece of paper into two columns. In the right-hand column, he transcribes a conversation in which he participated. In the left-hand column, he writes what he was thinking and feeling but didn't express at each point during the exchange. "Joe's Left-Hand/Right-Hand Columns" shows an excerpt from a conversation in which an executive confronted a manager about using inappropriate humor.

This exercise shows how unstated reasoning can be crafted just as defensively as stated reasoning, Argyris says. For instance, the comments in a person's left-hand column often attribute ill intent to the other conversation participant. Rather than writing statements such as "I've clearly made a mistake here" in their left-

Joe's Left-Hand/Right-Hand Columns

What Joe thought or felt but didn't express during his conversation with Bill	What Joe and Bill actually said to each other
	Joe: Some employees are upset about offensive jokes you've made.
He's not concerned about this. He doesn't understand the tension he's causing among the staff.	**Bill:** Don't worry—I'm always appropriate. They understand I'm just joking. If they were really upset, they'd tell me. Who's upset?
I'm afraid he'll confront the staff if he feels threatened.	**Joe:** I don't think they feel comfortable discussing this with you directly.

hand column, people blame others for problems under discussion.

"This exercise can help people see how defensive their thinking really is," Argyris maintains, "and how this kind of thinking gums up their exchanges at work."

3. Balance advocacy and inquiry

The key to replacing those defensive routines you detect is to open conclusions, claims, and opinions to testing.

Balancing advocacy and inquiry can help. With advocacy, you explain what led you to arrive at your conclusion. With inquiry, you ask for confirmation or disconfirmation of what you've said and invite others to explain how they arrived at their conclusion. Here's an example:

Marya: Ted, I know you believe that our company needs to develop new markets, but I disagree. Here's why. [She cites a specific example from another company or explains the assumptions behind her opinion—her belief that a company should enter new markets only after it has reached a certain size.]

Ted: Well, I can see now why you disagree.

Marya: What do you think of the explanations I've offered? Do they make sense?

Ted: I'm not sure you can draw an analogy between our company and that one. We're operating under very different conditions.

Marya: What makes you say that?

Balancing advocacy with inquiry—and helping others to do the same—can expose ideas to challenge and break the self-referential quality that characterizes much defensive reasoning. But as Argyris points out, you have to genuinely want to hear the answers to your inquiries. If you only pay lip service to inquiry—inviting others to challenge you but then not listening to them or punishing them—you'll embed defensive reasoning more firmly in your company or unit.

4. Identify defensive reasoning

Don't shy away from pointing out defensive reasoning that persists despite attempts to root it out. For example, suppose you disagree with a suggestion that Simon, a marketing manager, recently made to adopt a new customer relationship management system. You want him to explain how he arrived at his conclusion that the new system would be a good idea. Simon responds with eva-

> You have to genuinely want to hear the answers to your inquiries.

sive answers or repeats his earlier comments advocating the proposed system. ("Don't worry—this is the cutting-edge stuff we need. And the vendor is top quality.")

In this case, you might say, "You seem to think that this is our best option for managing our customers. But it's hard for me to learn about the possible risks of this idea from your responses. And I can't help you examine possible downsides. You haven't explained your thinking or invited me to inquire into it. So I can't test the validity of what you're saying. At this point, all I can do is accept your word that this system is the way to go. And I'm not willing to do that."

5. Be a model

Eradicating defensive routines must start at the top of an organization, says Argyris. If a powerful leader starts communicating more productively, a few people will notice and be inspired to make similar changes. The impact of their new behavior will then spread further out in the organization.

Though defensive routines will always exist in organizations, executives and managers can combat the worst of their consequences by recognizing the symptoms and modeling more productive ways of thinking and communicating.

Reprint U0503D

Better Decisions?

Keep Your "Lizard Brain" in Check

* * *

Loren Gary

Advanced cortical functioning is what separates human beings from the rest of the animal world, but our synaptic networks can betray us just when we need them most. Say we need to make a rational decision. Suddenly our "lizard brains"—the mental processes that tell us to flee or fight, panic or protect our turf—may take over. Result: fear or aggression dominate the decision, and we don't know why. "Managers may not even be conscious of how their lizard brains are controlling their thinking," says Richard Gooding, a management consultant.

To make decisions like a real *Homo sapiens,* advises Gooding, use a structured process. A good process keeps fears and political machinations in check. It prevents you from perseverating over details or putting the decision off until it's too late, and so minimizes the drain of decision making on time and morale.

There are plenty of good decision-making processes around, and it may not matter much which you choose. But the process outlined in the book *Smart Choices* may be as good as any. Authors John S. Hammond, Ralph L. Keeney, and Howard Raiffa focus on eight key activities: defining the right problem, specifying objectives, generating imaginative alternatives, assessing the consequences, weighing tradeoffs, identifying the areas of uncertainty, factoring in your tolerance for risk, and sequencing your decision making so that the decisions you reach today will make future decisions easier.

They also offer a series of diagnostic questions to guide you through each step. Take "defining the right problem." Ask yourself not only what the broad decision is that you must make, but also what smaller, more specific decisions are part of that broad decision. If your best path of action isn't clear, figure out what's making you hesitate about deciding now. Try to isolate the critical issues, then assemble any data or opinions that will make the decision easier.

But since no process is foolproof, keep the following tools handy as well:

Pretend you're running an emergency room.

If the decision facing you is simple, imagine you've got only a couple of minutes to determine a course of action. For a more complicated decision, give yourself a few hours.

Use a telephoto-lens technique.

After you've scanned the big-picture view of the problem, zoom in to assess how strategic decisions will affect tactics or operations. Then zoom back out to the strategic level to see if any adjustments are in order.

Let your mouth jump-start your mind.

If you get stuck, seek out a trusted colleague and talk things over; verbalizing your thought processes can help clarify connections you hadn't seen before. But use advisors for what they're good at—providing information about problem definitions, alternatives, consequences, and uncertainties. Rely on your own judgment where you know more than they do, advise the *Smart Choices* trio—for example, about your values and objectives.

Know when to quit.

Will your best choices disappear if you deliberate much longer? Would the perfect solution be only slightly better than your current best alternative, and would pursuing it detract from other important activities? If your answer to any of these is yes, your deliberation is done.

Don't underestimate group consensus.

Even if your group hasn't decided on all ten issues that need to be resolved, get started on the ones that everyone agrees are the highest priorities.

Setting up a structured decision-making process may seem like a lot of work, Gooding acknowledges, but it pays for itself. By freeing you from your lizard brain, it can help ensure your survival in the Darwinian jungle of business.

Combating Cognitive Biases

. . .

When making decisions, we all can fall prey to errors in our thinking process—what experts call cognitive biases. The articles in this section identify common types of biases and provide recommendations for recognizing and avoiding them.

Examples of biases include letting ourselves be most influenced by information that is vivid, recent, and easily retrievable, as well as seeking information that confirms the "wisdom" of a choice we've already made. Owing to another bias, we tend to rely too much on historical precedent to guide us while making decisions.

Common safeguards against cognitive biases include actively searching for data that disconfirms your conclusion, challenging historical precedents that have become so ingrained that they're no longer questioned, and waiting a few days before acting on a choice you've made, so you can be certain it's appropriate.

Cognitive Bias

Systematic Errors in Decision Making

• • •

Loren Gary

A December 1997 article in *Harvard Management Update* described a purely rational approach to decision making. In real-world situations, however, managers' decision-making processes regularly fall short of this ideal. Nobel laureate Herbert Simon demonstrated 40 years ago that purely rational judgment is "bounded" by insufficient information about the definition of the problem and the relevant criteria, time and cost constraints on the quality and amount of data available, as well as by mental and perceptual constraints that inhibit decision makers' ability to determine the optimal choice. As a result, writes Max Bazerman, J. Jay Gerber Distinguished Professor of Dispute Resolution and Organization at Northwestern's Kellogg Graduate School of Management, decision makers "forego the best solution in favor of one that is acceptable or reasonable." To use the term Simon coined to describe these shortcuts, they *satisfice.*

Fifteen years after Simon published his work on bounded rationality, Amos Tversky and Daniel Kahneman produced an analysis of specific systematic biases, or simplifying strategies, that affect judgment. These strategies, known as *heuristics,* are "the standard rules that implicitly direct our judgment," explains Bazerman in *Judgment in Managerial Decision Making.* "They serve as a mechanism for coping with the complex environment surrounding our decisions."

Empirical research has identified "13 specific biases that affect the judgment of virtually all managers," Bazerman continues. Summarized in the accompanying table, these biases derive largely from three more general heuristics: the availability heuristic, the representativeness heuristic, and anchoring and adjustment.

On average, the use of judgment heuristics produces far more adequate than inadequate decisions. Most of the time, however, we are oblivious to these heuristics and their impact on our decision making—and that lack of awareness can lead to trouble.

The Availability Heuristic

"An event that evokes emotions and is vivid, easily imagined, and specific will be more 'available' from memory than will an event that is unemotional in nature, bland, difficult to imagine, or vague," declares Bazerman. "For example, the subordinate in close proximity to the manager's office will receive a more critical performance evaluation at year-end, since the manager is more aware of this subordinate's errors." Although this heuristic often produces accurate judgments, its fallibility lies in the fact that the availability of information about an event is also affected by other factors unrelated to the event being evaluated.

Three biases result from the availability heuristic: *ease of recall, retrievability,* and *presumed associations.* Take the ease-of-recall bias; purchasing behavior has been shown to be influenced by the vividness and frequency of the advertising message. Operating from memory, consumers often buy an inferior product because it's the one they remember.

The Representativeness Heuristic

This category of cognitive bias, observes Bazerman, results from managers assessing "the likelihood of an event's occurrence by the similarity of that occurrence to their stereotypes of similar occurrences." Thus, a manager may predict the success of a brand extension because of its resemblance to past successful extensions. This heuristic can lead to a "good first-cut approximation," Bazerman acknowledges, but relying on it when the information is insufficient will lead to miscalculations.

Summary of the Thirteen Cognitive Biases

Biases Emanating from the Availability Heuristic

Ease of Recall

Individuals judge events that are more easily recalled from memory, based on vividness or recency, to be more numerous than events of equal frequency whose instances are less easily recalled.

Retrievability

Individuals are biased in their assessments of the frequency of events based on how their memory structures affect the search process.

Presumed Associations

Individuals tend to overestimate the probabilities of two events co-occurring based on the number of similar associations that are easily recalled, whether from experience or social influence.

Biases Emanating from the Representativeness Heuristic

Insensitivity to Base Rates

Individuals tend to ignore base rates in assessing the likelihood of events when any other descriptive information is provided—even if it is irrelevant.

Insensitivity to Sample Size

Individuals frequently fail to appreciate the role of sample size in assessing the reliability of sample information.

Misconceptions of Chance

Individuals expect that a sequence of data generated by a random process will look "random," even when the sequence is too short for those expectations to be statistically valid.

Regression to the Mean

Individuals tend to ignore the fact that extreme events tend to regress to the mean on subsequent trials.

The Conjunction Fallacy

Individuals falsely judge that conjunctions are more probable than a more global set of occurrences of which the conjunction is a subset.

Insufficient Anchor Adjustment

Individuals make estimates for values based upon an initial value (derived from past events, random assignment, or whatever information is available) and typically make insufficient adjustments from that anchor when establishing a final value.

Conjunctive and Disjunctive Events Bias

Individuals exhibit a bias toward overestimating the probability of conjunctive events and underestimating the probability of disjunctive events.

Overconfidence

Individuals tend to be overconfident of the infallibility of their judgments when answering moderately to extremely difficult questions.

Two More General Biases

The Confirmation Trap

Individuals tend to seek confirmatory information for what they think is true and neglect the search for disconfirmatory evidence.

Hindsight and the Curse of Knowledge

After finding out whether or not an event occurred, individuals tend to overestimate the degree to which they would have predicted the correct outcome. Furthermore, individuals fail to ignore information they possess that others do not when predicting others' behavior.

Biases emanating from the representativeness heuristic include *insensitivity to base rates, insensitivity to sample size, misconceptions of chance, regression to the mean,* and *the conjunction fallacy*. With the regression-to-the-mean bias, for example, we devise predictions "based on the assumption of perfect correlation with past data," Bazerman explains. That is, we may predict a certain sales volume for 1998 because we believe the sales experience for 1997 will be completely predictive—when, in fact, it is likely to be only partially predictive.

Or consider the conjunction fallacy. While simple statistics, writes Bazerman, can show that "a conjunction (a combination of two or more descriptors) cannot be more probable than any one of its descriptors, the conjunction fallacy predicts and demonstrates that a conjunction will be judged more probable than a single component descriptor when the conjunction appears more representative than the component descriptor." Thus, in a study conducted in July of 1982, experts evaluated "the probability of a complete suspension of diplomatic relations between the United States and the Soviet Union some time in 1983 to be *less likely* than the probability of a Russian invasion of Poland and a complete suspension of diplomatic relations" between the U.S. and the USSR.

Anchoring and Adjustment

"Managers make assessments by starting from an initial value and adjusting to yield a final decision," Bazerman writes. "The initial value, or starting point, may be suggested from historical precedent, from the way in which a problem is presented, or from random information. . . . In ambiguous situations, a trivial factor can have a profound effect on our decision if it serves as the starting point from which we make adjustments."

One of the biases that results from anchoring and adjustment is *insufficient anchor adjustment*. For example, a compensation system that awards an average increase of 5% to all employees can lead to inequities if some employees have been underpaid to begin with. Other biases that flow from anchoring and adjustment include the *conjunctive and disjunctive events bias*—we tend to overestimate the probability of events that must occur in conjunction with one another and underestimate the probability of disjunctive events, events that occur independently—and *overconfidence,* the tendency of decision makers to be, in Bazerman's words, "most overconfident of the correctness of their answers when asked to respond to questions of moderate to extreme difficulty."

The last two biases are *the confirmation trap* and *hindsight and the curse of knowledge.* Seeking confirmatory evidence while excluding the search for disconfirming information is an example of how the confirmation trap inserts itself into the decision-making process. Hindsight, writes Bazerman, refers to the research finding that "knowledge of an outcome increases an individual's belief about the degree to which he or she would have predicted that outcome without the benefit of that knowledge." The curse of knowledge is a phenomenon related to hindsight. In this instance, "knowledge that is psychologically available is hard to forget when a person is imagining how much others know"—which explains why technical writers regularly overestimate the average person's ability to understand software-instruction manuals.

The key to improved judgment, writes Bazerman, "lies in learning to distinguish between appropriate and inappropriate uses of heuristics." But it isn't getting any easier to accomplish that, says Quinn Spitzer, chairman and CEO of the management consulting firm Kepner-Tregoe. The coauthor of *Heads You Win,* Spitzer maintains that "there is anecdotal as well as empirical evidence that the quality of managerial decision making is declining." Citing a 1996 Reuters study that showed managers are being called upon to sift through increasing amounts of information and at the same time having to make decisions more rapidly, he lists three reasons for the decline.

"When the time frame for decision making becomes short, there's a lack of attention to process—which allows all the judgment biases to come into play. We're also finding a decline in data integrity. Your decision is only as good as the quality of information you're dealing with; the larger the data set, the harder it becomes to distinguish fact from perception. Moreover, the data sets themselves are changing. Implementation of decisions tends to be slowed nowadays, often because one decision is chained to a number of other decisions. So from the time a decision is made to the time you're ready for implementation, the relevant data could have changed—the original conditions might no longer apply."

Even when you're in a time crunch, it's wise to take a moment to look at the larger decision landscape. Is the decision you've been presented actually the most important one you need to make right now? Are there other key decisions that are linked to this one? If so, what are the precedence relationships, that is, how do those decisions need to be sequenced? But the most important thing is to have "a transparent decision-making process," advises Spitzer. "People in a company will probably disagree about whether there is sufficient, reliable data to support a particular decision, but with a transparent process they can still communicate with one another, explain their assumptions to one another."

For Further Reading

Judgment in Managerial Decision Making by Max Bazerman (4th ed., 1998, John Wiley & Sons)

Heads You Win: How the Best Companies Think by Quinn Spitzer and Ronald Evans (1997, Simon & Schuster)

"Judgment Under Uncertainty: Heuristics and Biases" by Amos Tversky and Daniel Kahneman (*Science*, Vol. 185, 1974)

Reprint U9804B

Cognitive Bias in Everyday Strategic Planning

• • •

Loren Gary

Fast-cycle decision making is about learning to pedal faster, but not exclusively so. It's also about redesigning the derailleur so that your company can make better decisions. The company that focuses obsessively on achieving breakneck speed, neglecting its decision-making processes, is headed for a crash.

An April 1998 *Harvard Management Update* article examining judgment heuristics—simplifying strategies, or decision-making shortcuts—left some readers with the impression that cognitive biases, the faulty patterns of thought resulting in the misapplication of judgment heuristics, are esoteric phenomena managers rarely encounter. Nothing could be further from the truth. Cognitive biases are, in fact, a lot like kudzu: they are introduced for the best of reasons, but then quickly threaten to take over the entire managerial landscape.

Strategic growth initiatives—new-product development, alliances, and mergers and acquisitions—seem especially prone to these unconscious errors in judgment. The bias creeps in unawares, becoming evident only in hindsight, in the light of some disastrous consequence. Three frequently encountered scenarios follow—each one illustrating a different cognitive bias—along with commentary from expert practitioners about how to avoid the decision-making error involved.

New-Product Development and the Confirmation Bias

The confirmation bias results when managers seek confirming evidence for what they think is true, or for the outcome they want to achieve, but neglect the search for disconfirming evidence. This bias comes into play in new-product development, says Richard Gooding, president of Strategic Advantage, Inc., when companies forget to "look at why the customer might not want the product that's being designed." Citing the example of Arizona Instruments, Gooding notes that the board of directors started pressing for a new product line not long after the company went public in 1989. "They came upon a new process for detecting underground gas leaks that was about 100 times more accurate than any existing technology. At the same time, the Environmental Protection Agency was getting legislation through Congress mandating that all underground gasoline storage tanks be continuously tested. So the thinking at Arizona Instruments was that it was going to introduce this superior technology at a time when an enormous demand for it was coming on line.

"The company sold its first installation incorporating the new technology in 1991—and that was the only unit it ever sold. The CEO acknowledged later that Arizona Instruments never put itself in the shoes of one of the intended customers for this technology—a Texaco or Conoco—and asked, 'How badly do we want to detect leaks in our underground gasoline storage tanks?' The answer, of course, was that they didn't want to know very badly at all—they just wanted to stay out of trouble with the Environmental Protection Agency. The technology that Arizona Instruments had developed could detect a leak the size of a glass of water from a 90,000-gallon tank. But EPA regulations allowed tanks of that size to leak 1,500 gallons of gas." In other words, customers didn't need or want so sensitive an instrument—but Arizona Instruments never bothered to ask.

When the federal government passes legislation, it typically leaves enforcement up to the states, which means that implementation occurs slowly. In the case of the EPA legislation concerning underground gas tanks, Gooding recalls, "only 40% of the nation's gas stations were in compliance six to seven years after the legislation passed." Arizona Instruments neglected to study how such legislation gets implemented, so it failed to anticipate why demand for its technology would never come on line. Seduced by the capability of the technology itself, Gooding continues, "management could see only why customers would be so excited to buy it."

The key to counteracting the confirmation bias in new-product development scenarios, says Gooding, who has been helping companies think about strategic growth initiatives for more than 18 years, is to "systematically get managers to take the opposite perspective. To put themselves in the customer's shoes and ask, 'Why might this product fail?'" Gooding facilitated such a conversation—he describes it as "a structured brainstorming process"—with Arizona Instruments some years later, when the company was planning to introduce a new moisture analyzer onto the market. "There were a number of issues that came up. Some related to reliability, quality, competitive response, equipment maintenance—60 or 70 items in all. But most interesting to me was the comment that it was just plain ugly—when I had the team prioritize the items, this one rose to the top. The team went back and redesigned the product inside and out. And it won an award for one of the 100 best products for 1997."

Strategic Alliances and the Availability Heuristic

Assuming that the most readily available information is the most pertinent information is an example of the availability heuristic. Biases that derive from this heuristic often crop up when companies are considering strategic alliances. A major reason for this, says Quinn Spitzer, chairman and CEO of the management consulting firm Kepner-Tregoe, is that "nobody is sure what strategic alliances are—they can range from a simple, circumscribed comarketing agreement all the way to a sharing of employees. Consequently, a 'collection phenomenon' often results": if one alliance is successful, managers will tend to say, "Let's do 20 more exactly like this one." The error, Spitzer continues, lies in the inference that the structure of the most recent alliance should govern all subsequent alliances—even when the needs of the companies involved are quite different.

The remedy for the availability bias, says Gooding, consists of "counteracting the natural tendency to look for confirming information" by broadening the information base. "The decision about a strategic alliance is often made by a pretty small team—three or four senior managers. I make sure to involve in the decision-making session more people than would typically be involved. The goal is to balance out the information and perspectives that different people have available to them, to bring to bear on the decision information that the senior managers may not have. Having more people present increases the likelihood of uncovering disconfirming information.

"But you can't treat all the perceptions as equals," Gooding emphasizes. "So it's critical to have the team prioritize the various comments. Then not only do you get all these different perspectives brought to bear, but you also get an overall rating of the importance of each particular issue. This ensures that the decision won't be driven just by who recalled what and how important they think it is. It will be driven by all these people recalling a broader set of issues and then systemically rating them based on a group discussion."

Mergers and Acquisitions and the Nonrational Escalation of Commitment

Our responses to decisions are influenced by the way we frame information, observes Max Bazerman in *Judgment in Managerial Decision Making*. But many managerial decisions, he writes, "concern a series of choices rather than an isolated decision. We are prone to a particular type of bias when decisions are approached serially—namely, a tendency to escalate commitment."

Potential mergers and acquisitions are often ripe for just this kind of misjudgment, says Gooding. "Several years ago, the American Management Association did a study of mergers and acquisitions. The biggest surprise, respondents said, was that the process of integrating the accounting systems between the two companies took much longer than expected. Many companies thought it would take six months but it ended up taking two and a half years. Now, if you don't have the comptroller, or the head of the accounting department, on the team that's considering the acquisition, that fact may never come to light until it's too late."

The extensive due diligence required for a merger or acquisition makes many companies reluctant to conclude that they shouldn't proceed with the deal. "There's a phrase called 'deal heat,'" Gooding explains, "which describes the momentum that is created by such a process. It becomes impossible for the organization to turn back, even though they might think it's not the right deal. Things get exacerbated if there is a bidding war: a company gets wrapped up in the auction-like atmosphere and ends up paying too much for the acquisition." So it's not surprising, adds Spitzer, that "so many mergers end up being failures. Just look at the pharmaceutical industry—in almost every instance, the combined entity has ended up with less market share than the two independent ones." His conclusion? "The due diligence process creates false beliefs. It enables you to be tremendously emotive. You fall in love with a potential acquisition before fully considering the alternatives."

Questioning your basic assumptions. Cultivating

richer, more diverse sources of information and opinion. Resisting the impulse to be swept away by the emotional flood tide of the new product, technology, or acquisition candidate. In all three scenarios, countering the decision-making bias involves raising it to the level of conscious discussion. "You have to take the time to build a conscious decision-making process," says Spitzer. "Generally, people tend to adjust their objectives as the data relevant to the decision starts coming in. What we try to do with clients is to get them to be very intentional about when and why they're changing the substance and relative weights of the criteria they established at the outset."

For Further Reading

Heads You Win: How the Best Companies Think by Quinn Spitzer and Ronald Evans (1997, Simon & Schuster)

Judgment in Managerial Decision Making by Max Bazerman (4th ed., 1998, John Wiley & Sons)

Tying the Corporate Knot: An AMA Research Report on the Effects of Mergers and Acquisitions edited by Don Lee Bohl (1989, American Management Association)

Reprint U9808D

Why Do We Make Bad Decisions?

• • •

John Hintze

Should we have seen 9/11 coming? What about the Enron collapse? The signs were there; people pointed them out, but the appropriate steps were not taken by those in a position to do something. Why is this? Politics? Greed? Those certainly contributed, but there was something else at work, too: A failure of common sense in decision making.

Look more closely at the past accounting scandals. Accountants are charged with providing independent assessments of a client's financial condition. But major accounting firms provide many other services to their corporate clients, such as tax and technology consulting. It stands to reason that those other relationships weigh heavily on an auditor's ability to make audit-related decisions, especially in complex, gray areas. Superiors want to please the client, and common sense suggests that a negative audit is likely to shorten an accounting firm's relationship with a paying client, and not just in terms of auditing.

But this common-sense insight was largely overlooked, due in part to biases, often unconscious, that stem from ingrained cognitive forces at work in the decision makers—at the accounting firms, at the companies they audit, and even at regulatory agencies. Similar biases affect the decisions we all make every day. The key to overcoming them, experts say, is to understand and recognize them.

The human mind appears to follow "cognitive rules of thumb," leading people toward making decisions that follow what experience has taught them to be the easiest and quickest way to deal with issues, says Harvard Business School professor Max H. Bazerman, author of *Predictable Surprises*. That instills biases that sometimes can lead even very smart people to make mistakes. Other biases include downplaying the probable consequences of today's actions and engaging in reasoning that is ultimately self-serving. For example, Bazerman says, the social psychologist Michael Ross noted "that if you ask a husband and wife independently to tell you what percent of the household work they do, the combined number is 130%."

Likewise, accountants seeking stakes in bigger partnerships may fall victim to biases that lead them to interpret data in self-serving ways. And clearly those biases, wrapping individuals up in decision-making cocoons, can lead to serious mistakes in judgment.

Other Influences at Work

Robert B. Cialdini, author of *Influence: Science and Practice*, examines influence and how psychology affects it. He says that the "fundamental psychological principles that people live" and make decisions by can be radically altered by the simple twist of a phrase. He points to infomercial pioneer Colleen Szot, who tweaked the "Operators are waiting. Please call now" call-to-action line at the end of a NordicTrack glider system infomercial to "If operators are busy, please call again." The results were tremendous. "If operators are busy, it means that a lot of people 'just like me' have decided to do this," Cialdini says.

So how does that insight translate into leaders overcoming their ingrained biases? And how can it improve their decision making?

The first version of the infomercial's call-to-action line left viewers only with a cold directive and the image of operators exchanging gossip at the drinking fountain. The second version, however, implied there would be great demand for the product and created a broader decision-making dimension for the viewer, emphasizing that other buyers have also decided to buy the product. As a result, the decision-making power was distributed from one to many decision makers. And that, effectively, is what leaders must do. "Managers need to recognize that sometimes the most important information comes from the side, from peers," not from leaders trying to move the people who report to them, Cialdini says.

That also means leaders have to listen to their peers' and subordinates' opinions. Imagine if the head honchos at Enron or the FBI had listened to Sherron Watkin's or Coleen Rowley's concerns about organizational and operational weaknesses within their organizations. The nation's seventh-largest corporation in terms of market capitalization might not have collapsed, and the Twin Towers might still be standing today.

But ignoring criticism or dissent is all too human. "Once we have made an active, public, voluntary commitment to a course of action, we tend to see that choice as substantially more attractive and worthwhile than we did immediately before making that choice," Cialdini says. He points to a study in which race track bettors were surveyed 30 seconds before placing their bets and 30 seconds after. The participants judged the prospects of their horses winning as dramatically higher after they had placed their bets.

Accounting for Ambiguity

"When an individual has a vested interest to see ambiguous data in a certain way—and accounting data are often ambiguous—[he is] incapable of being objective," Bazerman says. In fact, he proposes that executives at any firm that wants repeat or additional business from a company are "no longer psychologically capable of rendering objective assessments" of that company's data.

In the accounting world, several options have been proposed to mitigate that ingrained tendency, including empowering the securities exchanges or the government to do audits, or limiting auditing firms to performing audits and requiring them to completely sever ties to clients after set time periods. The proposals seek to remove conflicts of interests. But no such extreme reforms were implemented by the Sarbanes-Oxley Act. It requires rotating auditors, for example, but only the individuals inside an accounting firm and not the accounting firm itself, so the conflicts of interest ultimately remain. And that's why Bazerman believes accounting scandals are bound to continue.

Accounting firms' conflicting client relationships were recognized years ago. In the mid-1990s, for example, then–SEC Commissioner Arthur Leavitt pursued putting more distance between auditors and their consulting arms but failed to introduce significant changes. There were even earlier accounting boondoggles, like the one perpetrated by Waste Management and its auditor, Arthur Andersen. But corporate management and accountants were already committed to the existing system, and those signs of percolating malfeasance simply weren't big enough to push them outside their decision-making cocoons.

In his new book, Bazerman argues that "surprises" like Enron and WorldCom are surprises only in terms of their specificity; that some companies would commit accounting fraud was entirely predictable, given earlier telltale signs. "When we have a clear need to act and we fail to act, and then one of the multiple things that could go wrong does, that's a predictable surprise," Bazerman says.

> That some companies would commit accounting fraud was entirely predictable.

Bazerman adds that he and George Loewenstein, a professor in the Department of Social and Decision Sciences at Carnegie Mellon University, told the SEC in the summer of 2000 that corporate failures stemming from auditor independence issues would continue unless adequate reforms were made. The SEC, however, asked for comprehensive evidence that consulting services corrupted audits—the proverbial smoking gun.

Likewise, the first draft of a Gore Commission report in 1996 sounded a clear call to action in terms of bolstering security at airports, but the passage in subsequent drafts was watered down. As issues build, says Bazerman, there is usually a small group that doesn't want to fix problems. The profit-hungry accounting firms' lobbying efforts to thwart reforms set the stage for recent accounting scandals, and the airlines, loath to spend more money to beef up security, left themselves exposed to the perpetrators of 9/11. But there is also a more general fear to act among those persons positioned to make potentially corrective decisions.

"What I think happens is that we're unwilling to have the courage to invest now, when nobody gives you credit for stopping a problem that they haven't ever seen," Bazerman says.

Also part of the problem is that industry and political leaders caught up in the fray have biases that allow them to set aside criticism. Plus, their staff may hesitate to deliver bad news. To avoid falling into that trap, Cialdini says, leaders must set up mechanisms that foster internal debate and endow their subordinates with powers that appear special. Doing so will spur reciprocity from subordinates, encouraging them to make decisions that benefit their boss and the organization.

Sidestepping Common Pitfalls

To avoid falling into the biased-decisions trap, Bazerman recommends that managers engage in more decision-making training. Recognizing where systematic biases lie can help prevent poor decisions. Bazerman also suggests that managers routinely audit their own decision-making processes, perhaps against a checklist of common snafus. When corporate leaders, for example, sign agreements with other companies, their biases can often lead them to gloss over ambiguities in the contract language, setting the stage for a predictable surprise later on. "What they're really guilty of is not eliminating the predictable surprise by creating clarity in the agreement to begin with," Bazerman says.

And finally, since Bazerman simply doesn't trust the mind to be "debiased," he recommends implementing structural measures that enforce room for independent thought.

"Some couples have a rule, 'We don't buy anything off of the TV without thinking about it for 24 hours and talking to each other,'" he says.

Reprint U0307C

How Good Data Leads to Bad Decisions

• • •

David Stauffer

The 1994 purchase of Snapple by Chicago-based food giant Quaker Oats appeared to be a no-brainer. CEO William Smithburg had engineered Quaker's spectacularly successful 1983 buyout of the slumping sports-drink company Gatorade, amid grave doubts expressed by industry analysts. With the Gatorade win behind him—he paid $220 million for the company and grew it into a business worth $3 billion—he seemed to have a gift for identifying smart buys. So the Quaker board gave him the go-ahead on the Snapple deal.

But that acquisition proved to be one of the most unsuccessful in American corporate history. It also cost Smithburg his job. Quaker unloaded Snapple in 1997 for $300 million, having paid $1.8 billion for it.

How could the Snapple purchase have gone so wrong after Gatorade had gone so right? The answer lies in our very human tendency to rely on historical precedent. It's in our DNA to seek help with today's decisions by recalling past decisions in situations that seem analogous. Only too late—and sometimes never—do we see that the earlier situation was quite different in fundamental ways.

Where do we err? We misremember. We remember selectively. We recall what's recent and neglect what's more distant. Or we recall what's traumatic and ignore what's subtle. "Where you stand today dictates what you see in the past," says Paul C. Nutt, author of *Why Decisions Fail* and professor of management sciences at Ohio State University. Thus, he notes, Quaker seems to have decided to purchase Snapple because it attributed the success of the Gatorade buyout largely to Smithburg's insight rather than to its actual basis: good luck.

Making a decision based on historical precedent has numerous pitfalls. But if you're thinking you're better off not to factor in any memories—forget it. Research shows that you'll consider past experience subconsciously, even if you disregard it overtly.

Fortunately, we aren't doomed to use historical precedent to misinform today's decisions. In fact, we need past events, experts say, to help us cope with the mind-boggling complexity of today's critical business decisions.

What's more, the beneficial use of past experience doesn't have to be a complicated or time-consuming effort. "You don't need a Ph.D. in decision making to be a little more orderly in making decisions," says John S. Hammond, head of his own decision-making consulting firm, and a former professor at Harvard Business School.

Here are the most important steps that decision-making experts recommend:

Cross-Examine Every Precedent

Subject the first historical precedent that occurs to you to a merciless barrage of validity tests. Research shows that the memory that bubbles up first is more likely than any other to steer you toward a bad decision. We're often unconsciously recalling a past event that confirms the decision we're already leaning toward.

"It's called the prism effect," explains Jack Beauregard, CEO of the consulting firm Innervisions Associates. "We only recall the analogy that confirms our present thinking."

Ernest H. Forman, professor of management science at George Washington University and coauthor of *Decision by Objectives,* concurs. "We're all prone to go with what worked out well," he says. And we're led even further astray if that past outcome, like Quaker's purchase of Gatorade, worked out by chance. "It's in your brain for the next 10 years" that your great insight produced the favorable result, says Forman. The top-of-mind recollection, once surfaced, tends to resist all logic that suggests its inapplicability. That's because the mind tends to overweight first thoughts and underweight subsequent evidence. This phenomenon is called "anchoring bias," says Hammond. "It's unbelievably powerful."

So how do you avoid it? "Look for disconfirming evidence," suggests Cornell University Graduate School of Management professor J. Edward Russo. "First, force yourself to list as many ways that your top-of-mind precedent is a mismatch as it is a match. Next, force yourself to come up with what at first seems to be a less similar precedent." Then try to list as many or more ways that it's a better match with your current decision than you listed for your first precedent.

The first precedent that comes to mind is often nearer in time to the current decision than it is closer in similarity. Get past this "recentness bias" by coming up with at least two events from the more distant past that seem in any way applicable, then follow Russo's advice to try to make them work better.

President John F. Kennedy battled recentness bias by having his aides read a history of World War I, says John C. Mowen, professor of marketing at Oklahoma State University, Stillwater. "JFK's intent was to get them thinking of precedents other than those arising from World War II," which they all had lived through and in which many, including the president, had fought.

Kennedy's successor, Lyndon Johnson, might have avoided the quagmire of the Vietnam War had he tested the top-of-mind precedent. "As an exercise, take the exact opposite view that memory presents," advises Fred Turner, a visiting scholar in communication at Stanford University and author of *Echoes of Combat: Trauma, Memory, and the Vietnam War.* That would have meant that the Johnson administration "would have considered whether their enemy, rather than they, had the popular support of the people—which we now know would have been a correct assumption."

Clearly, emotion and personal attachment loom large in dictating the historical precedent that most readily comes to mind. Another way to soften the outsize impact is to introduce more-objective decision-making criteria, a tack recommended by The GenSight Group. "This helps you get the emotion and opinion out of recollections of past experience," says Jon Donnelly, vice president of strategic planning and process excellence for Janssen Pharmaceutica, a unit of Johnson & Johnson that has started to implement decision processes suggested by GenSight.

"Much more often than not," says Donnelly, eliminating emotion and opinion also eliminates the supposedly analogous precedent in its entirety. "Suppose we are faced with alternative investments to either expand a sales force or invest in additional clinical trials. A decision maker who was once a field sales manager or a clinical director might base his recommendation on his experience of five or six years ago. That might have been a big factor—literally decisive—in a traditional environment. We consider many factors today—both financial and strategic. As it is, the former sales manager or clinical director is as likely as anyone to eventually see that the precedent's current applicability is minimal or non-existent."

Require Proof of Common Knowledge

"Memory is contrived and re-created to suit our current needs," observes GenSight Group President Michael Menard. So apply factual research to the historical precedent that's so widely accepted in an organization that it's no longer challenged. Things deemed to be common knowledge are often the result of inferences made by the "primal" mind—they're a product of evolution, and so tend to be governed by emotions and instinct.

"We can't reverse evolution, but we can use our 'analytical' mind to understand and better cope with the ways evolution causes us to think," Menard continues. An essential part of applying our analytical mind in decision making "is to collect, manage, and visualize relevant data."

"The beauty of being able to display data is that it can

be very objective," says Todd D. Render, director of research and development for DePuy Orthopaedics, another unit of Johnson & Johnson that is implementing GenSight's decision processes. "You can display multiple factors, such as risk and expectations, in ways that make choices obvious to decision makers."

Render acknowledges that he can't quantify bottom-line benefits to the company of the new decision process. "But what I can say is that everyone—marketing, development, operations, and so forth—has input and everyone communicates. I think those may be our biggest gains. I'm certain we're getting better-quality decisions because we're using better inputs."

Those inputs need not be sophisticated or extensive. "Gathering data doesn't mean you study a decision to death," says consultant Larraine Segil, a former aerospace company CEO who is founding partner of The Lared Group, a strategic alliance advisory firm. "What's important is doing some cognitive screening, which can get us sufficiently disentangled from our past experience to assess it intellectually."

Encourage Others to Challenge Your Thinking

The relevance of a particular historical precedent can be more solidly established if you invite others to comment on its validity—others who feel free to dismiss the past events you may consider significant. Just be careful that you don't restrict their comments. Says Forman: "Many CEOs ask for a briefing: 'Just give it to me in a nutshell.' You can't fit very much in a nutshell."

In general, the more people challenging your precedents and suggesting their own, the better, Forman continues, "particularly if they're people with motivations different from yours." Sometimes, however, the decision-making group can turn into a "BOGSAT" (bunch of old guys/gals sitting around talking). Such a bunch is highly prone to "groupthink," a term popularized by the late decision researcher Irving L. Janis in his classic 1982 book, *Groupthink*. Janis demonstrates how decision making can go very wrong "when a 'we-feeling' of solidarity is running high" in a decision-making team and its members fall prey to "concurrence-seeking behavior."

> It's called thinking outside the box, where the box is all past experience.

The tendency toward decision biases, such as the recentness bias, increases when groups make decisions, as compared with when individuals do, says Oklahoma State's Mowen. "The dominant view will be enhanced as others participate." To counteract the tendency, "you need a devil's advocate," he says. "Among my five partners and me, at least one of us is playing devil's advocate for every significant decision," says James Segil, president and COO of enterprise software developer KnowledgeBase Solutions.

Turner approvingly calls the formal creation of a naysayer role an encouragement of "heretics and heretical thinking. Some people play that role intuitively," he says. "But in some large organizations, such as AT&T and Shell Oil, it's done intentionally, by design." Heretics also aid decision making by advocating radical departure from the path everyone else is taking. "They urge a contrarian decision. For example, if I were a venture capitalist right now, I might be investing heavily in dot-coms, because everyone else has fled that market following its traumatic meltdown."

Segil strongly endorses the contrarian approach. He launched his current enterprise just under two years ago, when the pervasive historical precedent looming over almost everyone's decision making was the dot-com crash. "It seemed to me to be the best time to start a business. Most people were too scared to do it. The few of us who did seem to be succeeding."

Never Rely Solely on Precedent

"History, contrary to the popular saying, never precisely repeats itself," Turner asserts. "Looking to the past can often limit the possibilities you see in the future."

He notes that Shell was the only major oil company to anticipate the oil price shock of the 1970s. Why? "Because their then-new scenario planning team considered the possibility of something everyone else thought impossible: that oil prices could shock." It's called thinking outside the box, where the box is all past experience.

Which is not to say that historic precedent should ever be completely discarded. Russo notes that some people do that, saying, "Everything's changed."

Above All, Develop a Process

Surprisingly, seat-of-the-pants decision making predicated on false or flimsy precedent occurs more frequently in today's sophisticated global economy than you might imagine. "We're shocked by the extent to which corporate America continues to ignore even the most basic practice of good decision making," says Menard.

For hope—and guidance—cast an eye toward Detroit and a long-standing paragon of American enterprise. There, a decision process being implemented at General Motors is built around something called a decision record. This document asks a few simple but critical questions about a decision, explains Nick Pudar, director of GM Strategic Initiatives. For example: What was the context of the decision? What was the decision? What resources were allocated? What alternatives were considered but not selected? Why? What assumptions were made? What outcome were you looking for? By when?

The document is completed and signed by the decision makers after a decision is reached but before it's implemented.

"It's quite an eye-opening experience," says Pudar. "People are forced to be clear. It can be painful. Decision makers will sometimes see the absence of substantiation staring at them from the page they filled out. But they can also solidify in their own minds exactly what they're deciding."

For Further Reading

Smart Choices: A Practical Guide to Making Better Decisions by John S. Hammond, Ralph L. Keeney, and Howard Raiffa (1998, Harvard Business School Press)

The Art of High-Stakes Decision-Making: Tough Calls in a Speed-Driven World by John Keith Murnighan and John C. Mowen (2001, Wiley)

Why Decisions Fail: Avoiding the Blunders and Traps That Lead to Debacles by Paul C. Nutt (2002, Berrett-Koehler)

Winning Decisions: Getting It Right the First Time by J. Edward Russo and Paul J. H. Schoemaker (2002, Currency)

Reprint U0212A

Leveraging Your Intuition

. . .

Intuition—the ability to know something without knowing *how* you know it—can help you make smarter decisions. And with today's brisk pace of change, many managers are relying more on their intuition to make time-sensitive business choices when they have scant information at hand. But the experts agree that, to get maximum value from your intuition, you need to improve its reliability.

The articles in this section offer guidelines for doing just that. For example, your intuition becomes more accurate when you have deep knowledge about the field in question. Therefore, building expertise by gaining ever more experience in a given field can help you strengthen your intuition's reliability. Keeping a diary in which you record your state of mind when you have intuitive thoughts can also help—by enabling you to eventually sort out intuitive thinking from thoughts based only on worries. And testing your hunches by discussing them with an unbiased friend or adviser can further enhance reliability.

Your Managerial Intuition

How Much Should You Trust It?

* * *

David Stauffer

The bad news about intuition is that there's no consensus on what it is, and no way to test the validity of an intuitive thought. The good news is that the bad news apparently doesn't prevent us from improving our intuition or benefiting from its use in making decisions.

What is intuition exactly?

You can't get far on the way to defining intuition without getting into an intellectual catfight. Weston H. Agor, a pioneer in studying the use of intuition in business decision making, says intuition is a kind of instinct. "We have neurological imprints just like birds' homing patterns," he observes. The implicit suggestion that what we know by intuition is something we never learned would raise eyebrows among a host of other researchers—for example, Paul J. H. Schoemaker, research director of the Huntsman Center at the Wharton School, chairman of the consulting firm Decision Strategies International, and co-author of the book *Decision Traps*. He acknowledges that "most people think of intuition as playing a hunch or going on gut instinct. But in decision research, we define intuition as an inability to articulate the thought process that led to a decision."

A chorus of boos would also greet any characterization of intuition as a psychic phenomenon. Cornell University psychology professor Thomas D. Gilovich, author of *How We Know What Isn't So,* notes that any claims involving the paranormal, by their nature, lie beyond the reach of evaluation and analysis. These and other hazards of defining intuition have led corporate attorney Richard M. Contino, author of *Trust Your Gut!,* to avoid "attaching labels to any thought process or belief system, because the act of labeling narrows our field of vision and our options."

Perhaps the best way to gain a measure of consensus is to say that intuition is at least, in the words of one writer, "knowing something without knowing how you know it" or, as in *Webster's New World Dictionary*, "the direct knowing of something without the conscious use of reasoning."

What makes intuition important to managers today?

However it's defined, there seems to be widespread perception that intuition plays a larger role in business decision making today than ever before, if for no other reason than that managers are increasingly forced to make decisions at a pace that allows too little time for analysis. As long ago as 1991, Agor, then a professor at the University of Texas at El Paso and head of the Global Intuition Network, perceived "a significant shift in the kind of decision and climate that organizations have to face. Decisions have to be much more rapid. And they're frequently made with inadequate information, because if you wait too long, you've lost your market." Plus, there is "a premium on the capacity to hear the first faint tap of a new trend."

Agor's thinking is echoed today by, among others, Joel

Yanowitz, managing director of Innovation Associates, a firm whose executive seminars for clients like Procter & Gamble focus in part on enhancing and applying intuitive skills. "Leaders today have to deal with multiple challenges and opportunities, develop compelling visions, and take effective action in a complex environment," he says. "Intuition is a necessary tool for tackling these and other imperatives. As such, we believe it's part of the skill set leaders need to be successful."

How reliable is intuition?

Among those who advise extreme caution in relying on an intuitive insight is Cornell University management professor J. Edward Russo, who conducts seminars on managerial decision making and is co-author (with Wharton's Schoemaker) of *Decision Traps*. In Russo's construct of intuition, "people match some characteristics of the current situation with similar aspects of a past situation, with no conscious awareness of the basis of the match. Intuition tells us to take the action in the current situation that either did produce or would have produced a successful outcome in the past situation."

But there's a big problem with acting on intuition, Russo continues: "The aspect or characteristic of the past situation on which we're matching may or may not have any relevance in the current situation. Your 'match' might be based on relevant or incidental parallels. Sometimes it will be one, sometimes the other." In other words, your bad intuitive feeling about a job candidate could stem from the fact that she, like a previous hire who didn't work out, grew up in Kansas. The similarity is irrelevant, but you don't know it's irrelevant because you aren't consciously aware of the basis of the match. "It feels right," Russo comments, "but there's no way for you to know if it *is* right."

Nonetheless, Russo doesn't say the unavailability of the previous "matching" situation to our conscious evaluation renders intuitive thoughts useless. "Consider your actions behind the wheel of a car today, versus when you were learning to drive. Back then, you had to think about every move you made; now it's automatic. The split second you save today by not having to go through a conscious thought process may mean you swerve or brake in time to avoid hitting another car."

Experienced managers, Russo allows, could certainly possess such "automatic expertise" in a variety of areas where they've worked. "But you have to ask yourself whether your past experience is pertinent in the current situation and, even if it is, whether that experience is still up to date." He illustrates with the example of a top officer of a pharmaceutical firm who rejected the sales program suggested by a market study. "He said, 'I was in sales for 15 years and I know doctors. My gut tells me they won't go for this.' The problem is that he was in sales 20 years ago, when he may have been right. But he doesn't realize that his automatic expertise is outdated;

and his marketing subordinates may not feel comfortable telling him that."

Russo's view of intuition as automatic expertise is supported by some research, such as that cited in a 1989 *Psychology Today* article, which noted that "researchers have found that intuitive people share one essential trait: They are experts in particular, if in some cases limited, fields of knowledge . . . Mastery of a field, these psychologists argue, is what makes intuitive thought possible."

"Mastery of a field" appears to be the one avenue that all observers agree can lead to the most consistently reliable flashes of intuition. This is the stuff of legend in sci-

> Mastery of a field is the royal road to reliable flashes of intuition.

ence and invention: the spontaneous blast of insight that shatters all real and imagined barriers to a monumental advance. Einstein himself is reported to have said, "I did not arrive at my understanding of the fundamental laws of the universe through my rational mind."

"We can trust the sort of intuition associated with scientific discovery," says Cornell's Gilovich. But he is skeptical of other claims attributing breakthrough thinking to intuition, such as the common assertion that wildly improbable entrepreneurial successes are achieved by people whose intuitive convictions prompted them to go against conventional wisdom. What's missing, he asserts, is a likely corollary: that many, if not most, such gambles fail quickly and quietly.

Contino agrees that intuition outside the realm of scientific inquiry can't be tested, but states, "untestable is not the same as dismissable. I have often seen business people who are bold enough to advocate a position based on intuition dismissed by other business people demanding data. They say, 'Forget your feeling, just tell me the facts.'"

Even the most enthusiastic advocates of intuition in business decision making say it's not smart to go only with intuition, unless time and circumstances totally preclude analysis. "You want to use both logic and intuition," Joel Yanowitz says. "I treat intuition as another form of data. Like any data, you ask if it's sufficient by itself to make a decision. For a major decision, it usually isn't sufficient, so you gather other data to test the validity of your intuitive thoughts."

How can you improve your intuition?

None of the experts or studies we consulted holds that we can't improve our intuitive thinking. Unfortunately, no single technique gains unanimous approval as a means of accomplishing this. The following list of steps represents the closest thing to a consensus.

Build expertise.

For those who assert that intuition flows only from mastery of a field, gaining ever more experience in a given area is the sole means of developing intuition. Wharton's Schoemaker, contending that intuition is "knowledge frozen into habit," observes that "you develop your ability to play intuitive golf, for example, by playing repeatedly and keeping track of results."

Remove distractions, get comfortable.

"People generally know the settings in which they tend to get their [intuitive] flashes," says Yanowitz of Innovation Associates. "For some it's a walk in the woods, for others it's driving the car, or listening to opera music. Put yourself in those situations to stimulate intuitive thought."

Keep a diary.

Attorney Contino says a diary "has made me more fully aware of my intuitive feelings and how much a part of my life these feelings are. It also serves as a record of my state of mind when I have intuitive thoughts, so I can now more readily encourage these thoughts by putting myself in similar situations." Yanowitz concurs, commenting that a journal or diary, over time, "can help you sort out thoughts that are in fact intuitive, as opposed to those based on worries or fears, or simply random."

Talk it over.

Cornell's Russo says that an intuitive feeling can sometimes be tested by "discussing options and preferences with an unbiased adviser or friend. A different perspective might indicate that either you're on the right track or you've been kidding yourself." Some observers advise that such a step be taken with someone completely outside the realm to which an intuitive thought applies. If the thought regards a work-related issue, for example, a discussion with a spouse or other family member might be in order. He or she probably has no hidden agenda and, being familiar with your behavior and thought processes, is likely to sense when your intuition is on the mark.

It's almost impossible to come up with a single summary recommendation for a topic as gelatinous and controversial as intuition in business decision making. But Innovation Associates' Yanowitz may come close when he warns, "You ignore intuition at your peril, and you follow it blindly at your peril."

For Further Reading

Decision Traps by Paul J. H. Schoemaker and J. Edward Russo (1990, Simon & Schuster)

How We Know What Isn't So by Thomas D. Gilovich (1993, Free Press)

Trust Your Gut! by Richard M. Contino (1996, AMACOM)

Reprint U9706A

"Decisions Don't Wait"

Talking with Andrew S. Grove

• • •

According to Andrew S. Grove, chairman and co-founder of Intel, when a company's understanding of itself shifts, when it changes its strategic paradigm, it sets out on a journey akin to moving from one mountain peak to another through what he calls a "valley of death." How do leaders sort through the confusion to identify the next peak that the company should be moving toward? When they're not sure where they're going, how can they guide and inspire others?

Grove, author most recently of *Swimming Across,* sat down with Harvard Business School professor Clayton

M. Christensen and with Walter Kiechel, editorial director of Harvard Business School Publishing, to discuss
these and other questions confronting business leaders
today.

**WK: You've spoken of high-tech companies,
Intel included, moving through a "valley of
death" right now. Where is Intel on its trek
through that?**

AG: Our last-generation growth has been fueled by a
fairly major structural transformation of the computing
industry from mainframe, centralized computing to distributed computing, PCs. And that defined the structure
for the entire industry, defined the growth opportunities, and defined the opportunities for packet software.

That framework is changing now. The Internet is
redefining software. The Internet is redefining the role of
computing and communication and their interaction
with each other. I still don't understand the new framework. I don't think any of us really do. But some aspects
of it are pretty clear. It's proven to be not computing
based but communications based. In it computing is
going to be subordinated to the communication task. It
is going to be very heavily dominated by the increasing
portion of all intellectual property being created in digital form, stored in this platform, and therefore ready to
be transported in digital form.

WK: Journeying from one business model to another is a formidable leadership challenge, especially in an industry so given to continual technological transformation. How do you handle that?

AG: None of us have a real understanding of where we are heading. I don't. I have senses about it. But decisions don't wait; investment decisions or personal decisions don't wait for that picture to be clarified. You have to make them when you have to make them. And try not to get too depressed in the journey, because there's a professional responsibility. If you are depressed, you can't motivate your staff to extraordinary measures. So you have to keep your own spirits up even though you well understand that you don't know what you're doing.

CC: If you look back in history at companies that have successfully launched new disruptive-growth businesses, with only a couple of exceptions, they were run by the founder. Is there something about being a founder that gives you the self-confidence to make an irrational or intuitive decision that goes against the logic of the organization?

AG: I've made the point about pretending confidence and building your own confidence in the face of this valley of death. If you implicitly believe that you have the support of the organization, above and below, by virtue of having been there for a long time and by virtue of people thinking that given that this is your baby—that what you're interested in is in the interest of the organization—that is more likely to happen if you're one of the founders or major investors, somebody's whose life is interwoven with the company. Secondarily—and this is a lot more complicated—if you are a founder of a business, you understand the business implicitly. You understand it through your skin.

If you are an outside manager, kind of a store-bought manager, you may be competent in a lot of things, but knowledge of the business is not what got you where you are. So you're less likely to have confidence in your own intuition. This is an intuitive process, because the numbers aren't in and the evidence isn't in.

CC: The problem with the way we teach is that if a student makes a comment in class that isn't grounded in the data in the case, the instructor is trained to crucify her right on the spot. And so we exalt the virtues of data-driven decision making. And then many of the students go to work for consulting firms where they carry data-driven analytical decision making to an nth degree. Thus, in many ways, the whole teaching model condemns managers to act after the game is over. Maybe you can't teach intuition, but maybe you can.

AG: You can promote intuition. You can recognize the innate aptitude of people to grasp what cannot be spelled out and cannot be shown by data, to be in tune with those vague attributes on the other side of that vague valley. And put them in positions where they can act on their intuition. But having said that, this presumes that the person making the promotion has a grasp of the situation. Which goes right back to where you started with your question. The senior leader has to have the understanding and the confidence in his conviction.

WK: Has a deference to the science of management gotten in the way of the art of leadership?

CC: I think the science of management wave already has been upon us for 20 years. I hope that we can figure out how to write and teach in a way that helps people develop an intuition for looking into the future clearly. If you only look into it through the lenses of the past, it's very hard.

AG: I think your question was asked in the context of business strategy. In that context, there is a problem between the scientific approach to strategy and the intuitive approach to strategy. But I don't think we should forget that there is more to running an enterprise, small or large, than strategy. The revolution in quality control and manufacturing techniques that has taken place in the last 15 years was data driven and systems driven and statistical process control driven. The U.S. economy has benefited incredibly over the last 15 years without a change in strategy, just by seriously embracing the science of manufacturing and quality control.

Figuring out what to do is important. But doing it and doing it well is equally important. And in the second category, the scientific, data-driven approach is absolutely well placed.

WK: We've been speaking of the founder's leadership; what about corporate leadership and the public's confidence in it in this era of accounting scandals? It seems that the entire corporate community is in its own valley of death right now.

CC: I have a theory of why we've had this spate of horrible accounting scandals. I pin the blame on economists, because they articulated the "principal-agent theory"; the idea is that the agents who are the managers of a company can't be trusted to carry out the wishes of the principals who own the stock, because their agendas are quite different. You have to align their incentives, which means heavily weight the compensation of the management team to stock options, so that what makes them rich makes the shareholders rich.

AG: The unstated supposition is that stock options are a means to solve the agency problem, to line up the interests of management with the owners or the top-level managers. When people who own 20% of a major public corporation give themselves 20 million share options, that flies right in the face of the principal-agent theory. You're going to tell me that when I own 20% of the shares, I don't act like an owner, I need 20 million shares to get me over my motivational hurdle?

When you have a company where practically all employees or professional employees or management employees are stock option holders or stock owners, their motivation in little increments is vectored closer to the interests of the company, and the whole organization works a lot better. So when you look at the use of stock options, and you look at companies that give 50% of their options to the top five officers, you get one picture. But when you look at companies where 90% or 95% of the options are given to people other than the top five officers, you get the other effect. So stock options are not the culprit. What you do with the stock options—who you give them to and in what amounts—is the variable that distinguishes how they work.

WK: Twenty million shares to a CEO—most people's question would be: Where was the board? You've been thinking about how to transform boards for a long time. Where's your thinking now?

AG: Well, bit by bit, under duress, boards are moving in the right direction. But where they started from is where they practically could be described as an advisory body to the CEO: selected by the CEO, working for the CEO, doing a certain amount of rubber-stamping of the CEO's actions, giving a bit of advice if things were going well—for most practical purposes, acting no different than a group of consultants or scientific advisers. Corporate governance is, or should be, exactly the other way around. The CEO is selected by, retained by, renewed by, and supervised by the board.

So you have the pro forma statement of what corporate governance is about, and you have the real-life workings of it. And the two have been diametrically opposite. There's a movement from this advisory-body model to the correct governance model, but with miles and miles to go. And a parameter of how many miles to go is the percentage of Fortune 500 companies where the chairman is a different person from the CEO—in 85% of the companies it's the same person.

If the chairman and the CEO are the same person, how the hell can the board of directors supervise the CEO?

Reprint U0301B

About the Contributors

Loren Gary is managing editor of *Compass* magazine at the Center for Public Leadership at the John F. Kennedy School of Government, Harvard University.

Fabian D'Souza, MD, MBA, is a Boston-based medical director with Integral, an international management consulting firm.

Jeffrey L. Seglin is an associate professor at Emerson College and author of *The Right Thing: Conscience, Profit, and Personal Responsibility in Today's Business* (Spiro Press, 2003).

Peter Jacobs is a freelance business writer based in Wellesley, MA.

Lauren Keller Johnson is a contributor to *Harvard Management Update.*

Adrian Slywotzky is a managing director of Mercer Management Consulting. He is also author of *How to Grow When Markets Don't* (Warner Business, 2003).

Paul Michelman is executive editor, HBR specialty publications.

Nick Morgan is a contributor to *Harvard Management Update.*

John Hintze is a New York-based writer of business and financial news.

David Stauffer is a writer based in Red Lodge, Montana.

Harvard Business Essentials

In the fast-paced world of business today, everyone needs a personal resource—a place to go for advice, coaching, background information, or answers. The Harvard Business Essentials series fits the bill. Concise and straightforward, these books provide highly practical advice for readers at all levels of experience. Whether you are a new manager interested in expanding your skills or an experienced executive looking to stay on top, these solution-oriented books give you the reliable tips and tools you need to improve your performance and get the job done. Harvard Business Essentials titles will quickly become your constant companions and trusted guides.

These books are priced at US$19.95, except as noted.
Price subject to change.

Title	Product #
Harvard Business Essentials: **Negotiation**	1113
Harvard Business Essentials: **Managing Creativity and Innovation**	1121
Harvard Business Essentials: **Managing Change and Transition**	8741
Harvard Business Essentials: **Hiring and Keeping the Best People**	875X
Harvard Business Essentials: **Finance for Managers**	8768
Harvard Business Essentials: **Business Communication**	113X
Harvard Business Essentials: **Manager's Toolkit ($24.95)**	2896
Harvard Business Essentials: **Managing Projects Large and Small**	3213
Harvard Business Essentials: **Creating Teams with an Edge**	290X
Harvard Business Essentials: **Entrepreneur's Toolkit**	4368
Harvard Business Essentials: **Coaching and Mentoring**	435X
Harvard Business Essentials: **Crisis Management**	4376
Harvard Business Essentials: **Time Management**	6336
Harvard Business Essentials: **Power, Influence, and Persuasion**	631X
Harvard Business Essentials: **Strategy**	6328
Harvard Business Essentials: **Decision Making**	7618
Harvard Business Essentials: **Marketer's Toolkit**	7626

The Results-Driven Manager

The Results-Driven Manager series collects timely articles from *Harvard Management Update* and *Harvard Management Communication Letter* to help senior to middle managers sharpen their skills, increase their effectiveness, and gain a competitive edge. Presented in a concise, accessible format to save managers valuable time, these books offer authoritative insights and techniques for improving job performance and achieving immediate results.

These books are priced at US$14.95
Price subject to change.

Title	Product #
The Results-Driven Manager:	
Face-to-Face Communications for Clarity and Impact	3477
The Results-Driven Manager:	
Managing Yourself for the Career You Want	3469
The Results-Driven Manager:	
Presentations That Persuade and Motivate	3493
The Results-Driven Manager: **Teams That Click**	3507
The Results-Driven Manager:	
Winning Negotiations That Preserve Relationships	3485
The Results-Driven Manager: **Dealing with Difficult People**	6344
The Results-Driven Manager: **Taking Control of Your Time**	6352
The Results-Driven Manager: **Getting People on Board**	6360
The Results-Driven Manager:	
Motivating People for Improved Performance	7790
The Results-Driven Manager: **Becoming an Effective Leader**	7804
The Results-Driven Manager:	
Managing Change to Reduce Resistance	7812
The Results-Driven Manager:	
Hiring Smart for Competitive Advantage	9726
The Results-Driven Manager:	
Retaining Your Best People	9734
The Results-Driven Manager:	
Business Etiquette for the New Workplace	9742

How to Order

Harvard Business School Press publications are available worldwide from your local bookseller or online retailer.
You can also call

1-800-668-6780

Our product consultants are available to help you
8:00 a.m.–6:00 p.m., Monday–Friday, Eastern Time.
Outside the U.S. and Canada, call: 617-783-7450
Please call about special discounts for quantities greater than ten.

You can order online at

www.HBSPress.org